When Media Succumbs to Rising Authoritarianism

This book provides a transversal scholarly exploration of the multiple changes exhibited around Venezuelan media during the Chávez regime. Bringing together a body of original research by key scholars in the field, the book looks at the different processes entailed by Chavismo's relationship with the media, extending their discussion beyond the boundaries of the specific cases or examples and into the entire articulation of a nearly-perfect communicational hegemony.

It explores the wide-ranging transformations in the national mediascape, such as how censorship of journalistic endeavors has impacted news consumption/production in the country to the complexities of Venezuelan filmmaking during Chavismo, from the symbolic postmortem persistence of Chávez to the profound transformations undergone by telenovelas, from the politically induced migration of online audiences to the reinvention of media spaces for cultural journalism as forms of resistance.

Allowing readers to engage not only with the particular case studies or exemplars presented, but with the underlying cultural, economic, political, societal, and technical aspects that come into play and which allow the extrapolation of this body of research onto other national or international contexts, this book will be an important resource for scholars and students of journalism, communication, media studies, and politics.

Ezequiel Korin is Assistant Professor at the University of Nevada – Reno.

Paromita Pain is Assistant Professor at the University of Nevada – Reno.

Routledge Focus on Journalism Studies

Metro Newspaper Journalists in China
The Aspiration-Frustration-Reconciliation Framework
Zhaoxi Liu

Drones and Journalism
How the media is making use of unmanned aerial vehicles
Phillip Chamberlain

The Rise and Fall of the British Press
Mick Temple

Toward a Theory of True Crime Narratives
A Textual Analysis
Ian Case Punnett

Peace Journalism in East Africa
A Manual for Media Practitioners
Edited by Fredrick Ogenga

Discourses of Legitimation in the News
The Case of the Economic Crisis in Greece
Vaia Doudaki and Angeliki Boubouka

Australian Sports Journalism
Power, Control and Threats
Peter English

When Media Succumbs to Rising Authoritarianism
Cautionary Tales from Venezuela's Recent History
Edited by Ezequiel Korin and Paromita Pain

When Media Succumbs to Rising Authoritarianism
Cautionary Tales from Venezuela's Recent History

**Edited by
Ezequiel Korin and Paromita Pain**

LONDON AND NEW YORK

First published 2021
by Routledge
2 Park Square, Milton Park, Abingdon, Oxon OX14 4RN

and by Routledge
52 Vanderbilt Avenue, New York, NY 10017

Routledge is an imprint of the Taylor & Francis Group, an informa business

© 2021 selection and editorial matter, Ezequiel Korin and Paromita Pain; individual chapters, the contributors

The right of Ezequiel Korin and Paromita Pain to be identified as the authors of the editorial material, and of the authors for their individual chapters, has been asserted in accordance with sections 77 and 78 of the Copyright, Designs and Patents Act 1988.

All rights reserved. No part of this book may be reprinted or reproduced or utilised in any form or by any electronic, mechanical, or other means, now known or hereafter invented, including photocopying and recording, or in any information storage or retrieval system, without permission in writing from the publishers.

Trademark notice: Product or corporate names may be trademarks or registered trademarks, and are used only for identification and explanation without intent to infringe.

British Library Cataloguing-in-Publication Data
A catalogue record for this book is available from the British Library

Library of Congress Cataloging-in-Publication Data
A catalog record has been requested for this book

ISBN: 978-0-367-61616-8 (hbk)
ISBN: 978-1-003-10572-5 (ebk)

Typeset in Times New Roman
by codeMantra

Contents

List of contributors   vii

Introduction: entering the forest without noticing the trees   1
EZEQUIEL KORIN AND PAROMITA PAIN

1   Two films: a rhizomatic connection   7
ARTURO SERRANO

2   Short-form documentaries, cyber activism, and resistance by Venezuelan filmmakers   20
CONCEPCIÓN CASCAJOSA-VIRINO AND BÁRBARA BARRIOS BARRETO

3   Asymmetrical information warfare in the Venezuelan contested media spaces   32
IRIA PUYOSA

4   Rebellious audiences: information platform migration and use of WhatsApp in a tyrannized society   46
CARMEN BEATRIZ FERNÁNDEZ

5   From riches to rags: the decline of Venezuelan telenovelas   61
CAROLINA ACOSTA-ALZURU

6   Status of institutional advertising in Venezuela during 1999–2018   77
AGRIVALCA CANELÓN S.

7 The return of the Caudillos in the digital
  age – changing hegemony and *Media Caesarism*:
  continuities and changes in the news media
  landscape under the *Chavismo*   90
  JAIRO LUGO-OCANDO AND ANDRÉS CAÑIZÁLEZ

8 Chávez's eyes: an iconic presence in the Venezuelan
  political communication   106
  MAX RÖMER-PIERETTI

9 Between resistance and reinvention: cultural diffusion
  in Venezuelan media   120
  MORAIMA GUANIPA

Index   137

Contributors

Carolina Acosta-Alzuru (Ph.D., University of Georgia) is Professor in the College of Journalism and Mass Communication at the University of Georgia, USA. She is the author of three books and multiple academic articles about telenovelas – a genre she has been studying since 1999. She is the recipient of the 2015 Scripps Howard Foundation Journalism and Mass Communication Teacher of the Year for the United States. In the last four years, her research has taken her to Istanbul as she examines the tensions between the domestic and global markets for Turkish dramas.

Bárbara Barrios Barreto holds a bachelor's degree in Audiovisual Media (with a Magna Cum Laude distinction) from Los Andes University (Venezuela). A freelance filmmaker, she holds a master's degree in Advertising Communication at Carlos III University (Spain), where she is currently a Ph.D. student researching about short films festivals as a launching platform for Latin American female directors.

Agrivalca Canelón S. (Ph.D., Universidad de Málaga) is the Director of the Master in Strategic Communication of the Faculty of Communication of the Universidad de La Sabana, Colombia. She holds a bachelor's degree in Social Communication (Print Journalism Mention), a master's degree in Social Communication (Organizational Communication Option) by Universidad Católica Andrés Bello in Caracas, Venezuela, and a Ph.D. in Organizational Communication by Universidad de Málaga, Spain. Her research areas include government communication, electoral advertising, public diplomacy, diaspora, and Venezuelan migration.

Andrés Cañizález (Ph.D., Universidad Simón Bolívar) is a senior researcher at Universidad Católica Andrés Bello in Venezuela. He is an author of several books and other publications on news media, political communication, and freedom of expression in Venezuela. Over the years, he has combined academia with the defense and promotion of human rights in Venezuela. His weekly analysis articles are published in five Venezuelan newspapers and news portals. He cooperates with projects of the People in Need NGO in Venezuela.

Concepción Cascajosa-Virino (Ph.D., Universidad de Sevilla) is Senior Lecturer at Carlos III University of Madrid, where she is a member of the research group TECMERIN and the director of the MFA in Screenwriting. She has written or edited nine books and more than 50 papers, including articles in *Studies in Hispanic Cinemas*, *Journal of Spanish Cultural Studies*, *Catalan Journal of Communication and Cultural Studies*, *Television and New Media*, and *Feminist Media Studies*.

Carmen Beatriz Fernández is a researcher and doctoral candidate at the Center for Internet Studies and Digital Life of the School of Communication at the University of Navarra (UNAV). She teaches Political Communication at IESA (Venezuela and Panama) and UNAV. She earned a Master in Business Administration (IESA, Venezuela) and Electoral Campaigning (University of Florida, USA). Mrs. Fernandez is the president of DataStrategia and cofounder of the Organization of Latin American Political Consultants OCPLA. She has been recognized with international awards such as: the Aristotle Excellence Award 2010 for her work in cyberpolitics, being part of the "Global Dream Team," the Eikon Regional 2013 for the best viral campaign, as well as several "Victory Awards" (2014–17) for influential women, academic excellence, and the best social network campaign.

Moraima Guanipa is Associate Professor and chair of the Journalism Department and a Humanities doctoral candidate at Universidad Central de Venezuela. Her research agenda is centered around the study of cultural information in print and digital media, the communicative expressions of art in cyber culture, and the challenges of professional development of journalists.

Ezequiel Korin (Ph.D., University of Georgia) is Assistant Professor of Spanish Language Media at the Reynolds School of Journalism of the University of Nevada, Reno. After many years of professional experience in various areas of communication in Venezuela, he joined academia upon completing his doctoral degree. His research addresses two areas: the use of digital technologies from the theoretical approach of critical and cultural studies and representation and identity of Spanish-speaking populations in American diasporas.

Jairo Lugo-Ocando (Ph.D., University of Sussex) is a Professor in Residence and Director of Executive and Graduate Education at Northwestern University in Qatar. He is the author of several books, dozens of journal articles, and other academic publications. Formerly to becoming an academic, he worked as a journalist and news editor for several newspapers in Venezuela.

Paromita Pain (PhD, University of Texas) is Assistant Professor of Global Media at the Reynolds School of Journalism of the University of Nevada, Reno. After several years working as a senior reporter in her native India, she joined academia, developing a rich and prolific research agenda around participatory media processes, citizen's journalism, and women's empowerment, as well as the impact of mobile technologies on news consumption.

Max Römer Pieretti (Ph.D., Universidad de La Laguna) is Professor at Universidad Camilo José Cela in Madrid, Spain, where he also has been serving as director of the Audiovisual Communication Degree since 2013. He was the director of the School of Communication (1997–2007) and the Director of the Graduate programs in Communication at Universidad Católica Andrés Bello in Caracas, Venezuela. His research agenda is centered around political semiotics and social media.

Iria Puyosa (Ph.D., University of Michigan) is a political communication scholar with highly specialized expertise in the field of information warfare in social media and political conflict in Latin America. Puyosa is Craig M. Cogut Visiting Professor 2019 at Brown University, where she advances research and teaches courses on networked social movements. She served as Chair of the Venezuelan Studies section of the Latin American Studies Association (LASA) 2018–20. She has worked as a faculty in universities in Colombia, Ecuador, Venezuela, and the USA, where she has taught courses on Political Communication, Media & Power, ICT & Politics, Civil Resistance, and Networked Social Movements. Her most recent publication is "Venezuelan Struggle Towards Democratization: The 2017 Civil Resistance Campaign."

Arturo Serrano (Ph.D., London University) is Assistant Professor of Film History at Universidad de las Artes (UARTES) in Ecuador.

He is currently the director of the Fuera de Campo film journal and is currently the vice director of the Universidad de las Artes Film School. He was a visiting scholar at the University of Maryland Film Department in 2013–14. He has authored "El sueño de la razón produce cine" (UCAB, 2011) and "El cine de Quentin Tarantino" (UCAB, 2014). His research intersects film history and cultural studies, both within and outside the Latin American context.

Introduction
Entering the forest without noticing the trees

Ezequiel Korin and Paromita Pain

Trying to understand any societal process spanning two decades is, in itself, a monumental task. This difficulty is further compounded by the high complexity of the Venezuelan situation, its antecedents and nuances, its highly politicized context and multidimensional characteristics. It is necessary, then, to parse out some of its constitutive elements in order to, later, rearticulate them into the conjunctural flux in which they gain relevance and produce significative effects.

During the past 20 years, Venezuela has undergone a fascinating – albeit highly problematic – political process. Within it, the relations between the group in dominance and the media have played a central role. In this period, Chavismo – the political current started by the late president Hugo Chávez – has understood the media as a premiere site for the articulation of a national consciousness and meaning-making, as noted by the government's unrelenting and overt attempts at establishing a communicational hegemony. To do so, Chavista governments have tried to harness the supersession of media representation above reality as a central element in their pursuit toward total control of public life in Venezuela.

But the tenuous relations between the late infantryman-turned-politician and the media predated Chávez's tumultuous presidency.

As institutions in their own right, Venezuelan private media corporations had been founded by powerful interest groups, several of which preserved sole ownership over an increasing array of outlets and channels, in the process amassing great political, financial, and cultural influence. Even within their ideological and political heterogeneity, for the most part, these media helped maintain and reproduce the dynamics of the status quo in the country prior to 1998.

Used to being deeply influential in national politics, a few Venezuelan media outlets openly supported the Chávez candidacy while others seemed set on an inevitable collision course. As such, during the run up to the 1998 presidential elections, some media reports painted a grim picture of then-candidate Chávez: one day, a video taken a couple of years before at the University of Havana made the news cycle; another day, another video, this time of a grainy tank attempting to run over a gate at Miraflores Palace during the Chávez-led 1992 failed coup made the rounds; later, it would be yet another video, this time belonging to the campaign trail, in which Chávez seemed to promise to deep fry the heads of some political foes.

The seemingly unrelenting barrage of damaging press would have been enough to upend – or, rather, end – any normal bid for the presidency within a democratic process. However, Chávez's rise to the presidency was anything but normal.

Chávez emerged as a response to a political system that had failed to effectively reinvest vast oil revenues in improving the lives of large swaths of the Venezuelan population. Greatly aided by an anti-left establishment backed by the United States since the mid-20th century, Venezuela had enjoyed the longest-running democracy in the continent. For nearly four decades, an informally established bipartisanship had nearly completely marginalized social movements demanding a more equitable redistribution of oil revenues and the improvement of societal conditions in the country. In the last presidential election of the 20th century, Chávez presented himself as the only viable option for the country to emerge from this slough: a political outsider who was unblemished, untouched, and unbridled by the innerworkings of the quagmire that had sunken Venezuela into the abyss of neoliberal policies that were to blame for the country's mishaps, or so the narrative went.

Chavismo's political positioning hinged on successfully articulating a dichotomic relationship with elements perceived as upholding the establishment – those that could be easily blamed for the country's misfortunes, those that would be pushing back against reforms billed as long overdue and necessary. Via this truly Manichean reductionism, it became possible for Chávez and his political movement to articulate and expand an "Us vs. Them" mentality that deeply resembled a tenet of fascism, under the guise of an inevitable class struggle.

This move would prove to be instrumental in defining the relationship between Chavismo and the media: first, via the dismissal of unfavorable news coverage as false reportages, media fabrications, political hit pieces, etc.; later, via the open contestation of the role played by media in shaping national culture and consciousness. While the former dynamic became the source of deep transformations to the country's legal scaffolding around media in general and journalism in

particular, the latter dynamic led to profound changes in the Venezuelan mediascape, either through direct government intervention and imposition or through less salient means such as obscure acquisitions of dissenting outlets.
Within this context, the relation between Chavismo and the media began taking shape. As such, the constitutional reform of 1999 – with great direct involvement by Chávez himself – included various articles that, while seemingly guaranteeing freedom of the press and preventing censorship, provided a legal anchorage for the penalization of information deemed not to be "timely" and/or "truthful." A series of legal actions and instruments, from anti-libel laws and onerous lawsuits to the assumption of the carrier's responsibility over the content that was transmitted, emerged from this scaffolding. A few years later, in an apparent exercise of the State's prerogatives regarding the use of the radioelectric spectrum, Radio Caracas Televisión's (RCTV) OTA television broadcast license renewal was denied. A few months later, hundreds of AM and FM radio stations across the country would be shut down due to administrative irregularities in their original licensing or in their subsequent renewals. Throughout the following years, similar discrete actions would continue to transform the Venezuelan mediascape.

Although many of these actions that helped shape the relationship between the media and the Venezuelan government under the direction of Hugo Chávez seemed to – at least – preserve the vise of legitimate State initiatives and responses, in time their combined outcomes led in a different direction. It is rather easy to point at the current state of the media in South American country from a highly critical and concerned perspective, as has been amply documented by national and international NGOs and institutions. What was challenging, if not outright impossible, was to foresee the extent to which the multiple discrete actions would, in sum, surmount to the erosion of democratic principles and the rise of authoritarianism in the country.

But how does the combination of small and, in many cases, seemingly innocuous actions end up producing such a dystopian situation around media and representation without setting off all the alarms?

In an attempt to answer this question, eleven authors explore how the Venezuelan government's actions during the past two decades deeply transformed the media and, in the process, set the groundwork for profound societal and cultural changes.

The gaze of the Venezuelan government is a constant and, as Max Römer-Pieretti articulates, the image of Chávez's eyes has been used to fuel public imagination ever since the electoral campaign of October

2012. This was done to keep alive the omnipresence of Hugo Chávez as guard of the revolution and ensure a dominant presence in political discourse in Venezuela, despite his death several years ago. Military uprisings, public mass protests, and even the possibility of US intervention have failed to undermine the current regime. Authors Jairo Lugo-Ocando and Andrés Cañizález explore how over the past two decades, the *Chavista* regime has been able to survive all attempts to oust it from power. What is central to this exercise of power? The authors suggest that the regime has successfully been able to build a new media and cultural hegemony that changed the terms of reference for many people in that country and this is what helps it beat any attempt to oust them from power.

The economic influence of the State as the main advertiser in the country certainly plays a role. Agrivalca Canelón S. uses the concept of the "Advertiser State," as proposed by García (2001), and "Myth of Government," by Riorda (2006), to extend our understanding of how authoritarian political regimes justify and legitimize their inherently autocratic character.

This is deeply reflected in the way culture is reported on and as Moraima Guanipa says, government actions have been oriented to the centralization and control of cultural activities as well as their coverage in the media. However, while the emergence of some private initiatives which foster greater plurality is also seen, the influences on cultural journalism have mostly been extremely negative, ranging from censorship to technological changes resulting in huge losses of readership.

The development and creation of this media structure happened over time and as Iria Puyosa says, the Venezuelan case offers a rare opportunity to analyze the information warfare promoted by a government in its evolution from illiberal democracy to authoritarian rule. Her study explores how as early as 2010, Venezuela's government pioneered the use of bots to foster trends on Twitter and the major online propaganda strategies used by the Venezuelan government on Twitter.

Audiences starved of information have turned to social media platforms for information and as Carmen Beatriz Fernández says, this migration from mainstream media highlights the importance of alternative channels. Her analysis suggests that in 2020 WhatsApp is the new destination for Venezuelan audiences seeking political information. Certain industries have felt the suppression more than others.

In Venezuela, the populist regime created a new communicational architecture, in which the new national media scheme clearly favored the official voice and its effects have been felt in every sphere of the media but perhaps, Venezuelan telenovelas have been the most impacted. In 1994, telenovelas were considered Venezuela's most important non-traditional export and a prosperous future was envisioned for this media product. As Carolina Acosta-Alzuru says, today no telenovelas are produced in Venezuela and the country's once powerful telenovela industry is virtually invisible in the international market. Her analysis based on research conducted since 1999 examines this deterioration, its causes, and consequences.

Like telenovelas, the crisis in Venezuela has restricted the development of the film industry as well and as Concepción Cascajosa-Virino and Bárbara Barrios Barreto say, in a process of increasingly violent social confrontation, some of these creators have chosen to become politically involved and take sides in the protest movements against the government of Nicolás Maduro, using film and social media platforms as a means and venue of protest. The authors analyze the short-form documentaries on YouTube, of Carlos Caridad Montero and Hernán Jabés, to assess how these two Venezuelan directors have adopted this type of activism and the impact of the transformation of traditional film practices, especially the migration to new media platforms to express opposition and protest the regime.

Film, with all its complexities of making, distributing, and exhibiting, continues to attract attention for their political significance in Venezuela's overtly politicized environment and Arturo Serrano shows how the story of two movies made in the same year about the same person, Simón Bolívar, can exhibit two distinct viewpoints. His study articulates, how films are a means of viewing history, as is public memory, but the truth is far more complicated than ether – simply because it is hardly black and white.

Through an in-depth analysis of these transformations in the Venezuelan media over the past two decades, this edited collection provides a starting point to understanding the complex articulations that have taken place and the far-reaching implications they have brought about in the Venezuelan society. In doing so, and despite its localized focus, it offers a cautionary tale of how media succumb to rising authoritarianism.

It is our hope that these texts will serve to better identify similar processes in other latitudes by providing a glimpse of the impending danger of forgetting that a forest is, ultimately, made up of multiple individual trees.

References

García, M. (2001). *Publicidad Institucional: el Estado Anunciante.* Universidad de Málaga.
Riorda, M. (2006). Hacia un modelo de comunicación gubernamental para el consenso. In D. Fernández, L. Elizalde & M. Riorda (Eds.), *La construcción del consenso. Gestión de la comunicación gubernamental* (pp. 17–142). La Crujía Ediciones.

1 Two films
A rhizomatic connection

Arturo Serrano

Abstract
Bolívar, el hombre de las dificultades and *The Liberator* were two films premiered one year apart. Right from the beginning, these films attracted a lot of attention for their supposedly opposing political views in an overtly politicized environment. In this chapter we show that the truth is much more complicated and that what these films show is how intricate cultural phenomena are in the context of the Bolivarian Revolution.

This analysis focuses on the complexities of making, distributing, and exhibiting cinema in Venezuela during Chavismo by concentrating on the story of two movies made in the same year about the same person. *Bolívar, el hombre de las dificultades* (Lamata, 2013) and *The Liberator* (Arvelo, 2013) premiered one year apart. Right from the beginning, these films attracted a lot of attention for their political significance in an overtly politicized environment. While Lamata's picture came with an official seal,[1] Arvelo's was widely viewed as an oppositionist film. The fact that both protagonists (Roque Valero and Edgar Ramírez) were very outspoken and politically active about their opposing political views helped in forming this point of view. While the protagonist of *Bolívar, el hombre de las dificultades* was a staunch supporter of Nicolás Maduro, Edgar Ramírez used every opportunity to make it very clear that he thought Chavismo had destroyed the country.

"Bolívar, two films, one epic?" (Straka, 2014) is the name given by the Venezuelan historian Tomás Straka to the most widely read critique about the two films. The reason for the name is that he wonders if those two films, which are supposed to be about the same person and therefore belong to the same epic, do indeed share it or if rather they show very concrete different and almost opposite views about Bolívar. Our title is inspired by Straka's title and in our case it refers to the fact that these two films are a perfect example of how complex the imbrication of cultural products is within the fiber of society, so much so that even in a case like this where the people involved seemed to have very clear opposing agendas, their films and the way they were distributed and exhibited show that they were the product of complicated political and cultural processes that "contaminate" everything.

I will try to show that even if in the collective imaginary there was a narrative in which *Bolívar, el hombre de las dificultades* and *El Libertador* were part of a much larger fight between Chavismo and the opposition, the truth is much more complicated. These two films do not support a black and white view. We will compare both films from the standpoint of the plot (how the films retell one point of view or the other) and distribution and exhibition (whether any of the films received or not favors from the government to favor its distribution).

Simón Bolívar, the "impossible character"

"¡Viva Bolívar! He aquí su rostro." With these words, spoken on July 24, 2012, President Hugo Chávez presented to the nation what the official press dubbed "the true face of Bolívar." The discourse of "the new" (the authentic which was going to be brought about by the Bolivarian Revolution) vs. "the old" (a false version sold to us by the corrupt Fourth Republic) was very popular among the official elite. Every opportunity was taken to rebrand what were considered the national symbols to impose a new way of seeing the country and its history. A good example is the rebranding of the flag in 2006 (a new white star was added to the seven already present on the color blue) and the modification of the Venezuelan coat of arms (the position of the white horse on the lower part was changed for it to face left).

But how could they rebrand Simón Bolívar? That was more difficult since Bolívar had always been an agglutinant character in Venezuela. In fact, his heroism, as told by the books, was in part an invention which served precisely the purpose to unite the nation and give it some sense of national identity.

To understand what Simón Bolívar means to Chavismo we need to go back to the beginning of the Revolución Bolivariana. As their ideological guidance and as a founding document to the political movement EBR-200, they chose what they called "the tree of the three roots." This tree is composed by Ezequiel Zamora (the E), Simón Bolívar (the B), and Simón Rodríguez (the R). And their project was defined as "the project of Simón Rodríguez, Master; Simón Bolívar, Leader; and Ezequiel Zamora, Sovereign General of the People" (Chávez, 2015: 43).

Just how important Bolívar was would become clear when Chávez proposed that the adjective "Bolivarian" be added to the name of the nation, thus changing it from "República de Venezuela" to "República Bolivariana de Venezuela." And the first article of the new Constitution reads that the values of the Nation are based "on the doctrine of Simón Bolívar, the Liberator." This was only the beginning of an attempt to completely appropriate Simón Bolívar at all levels in order to "use his figure, his thought and his actions as a strategy to propitiate and secure the divisions among Venezuelans in two highly polarized groups: the government's supporters and their opponents" (Chumaceiro, 2003).

The golden opportunity came in 2010 when Simón Bolívar's remains were exhumed from the Panteón Nacional to investigate whether he had been assassinated, as President Chávez suspected (Vinogradoff, 2010), or whether he had died of natural causes as the history books say. Besides the sleuth work that was going to be done to the body, a facial digital reconstruction of his face using the skull was ordered. All mentions in the press included information about what was dubbed a "scientific process" that had produced the image of "the true face of Bolívar," thus trying to give it an air of truth to go along with the aforementioned discourse on the authentic against the inauthentic or plainly false (Report on the 3D facial reconstruction of the Liberator Simón Bolívar, 2010).

When Hugo Chávez unveiled the said "true image of Bolívar" in 2012, Venezuelans held their breath in disbelief. The ubiquity of the image of the Father of the Fatherland makes Venezuelans very familiar with it. In 1872 President Guzmán Blanco created a law naming all main squares in all cities and towns "Plaza Bolívar" and a statue of the hero had to be placed in the middle of said squares. Also, by law, a portrait of Bolívar has to hang in all public offices and classrooms of the nation which is replicated by many private offices and shops. This attests to the fact that all Venezuelans feel they know Bolívar's image by heart. But in July 2012 a stranger stared back at us. Where was the man represented in the profile designed by Albert Désiré Barre and which adorned all Venezuelan coins since 1873? Was this image of the same man as the elegant and slender Bolívar of José Gil de Castro (image about which the "Libertador" himself said it had "the greatest accuracy and likeness") (Boulton, 1982)?

Representing the unrepresentable: cinematic representations of Simón Bolívar

The so-called "true face of Bolívar" is but one of many of the moments when depicting the Liberator has generated stir and controversy. To properly understand the two films, we are analyzing here, it is very important first to grasp how complicated cinematic representations of Bolívar have always been.

As a character Bolívar is as unapproachable and unrepresentable as in real life. In his book *El culto a Bolívar*, Carrera Damas develops the hypothesis that once the Venezuelan independence effort was completed came the great disappointment. The population had to face incredibly difficult circumstances which plunged them into great disappointment because "not only did they not see the promised reward coming, but felt it drift further and further" (Carrera, 2003: 43). This is why the need for a figure that would unite all Venezuelans in a common purpose arose. And that figure was Simón Bolívar. Thus, began the cult of the Liberator, which

> constituted a historical necessity, without that meaning more than what the concept of necessity can express in the historical order. Its function has been to simulate a failure and retard the lie. And up until now, it has fulfilled its duties satisfactorily.
>
> (Carrera, 2003: 42)

This cult made Bolívar a character of stories of heroes closer to Olympus than to Athens. This had consequences not only in the political, social, and economic world but also in the arts because when it came to represent the Liberator artists felt the heavy burden of responsibility on their shoulders. The world of cinema was no exception. As Rodolfo Izaguirre states, when it comes to Bolívar we are faced with a figure "impossible to access cinema screens" (Izaguirre, 1993: 73).

> Every time a project was announced, the tide of opinions whipped the pages of the publications: "The Liberator must not be allowed to be personified!", was one of the most frequent headlines in the press in Caracas during the fifties. Many people were involved in the debate... all of them coincidental in that a firm, zealous and patriotic vigilance should be maintained.
>
> (Izaguirre, 1993: 71)

It is fair to say that Venezuela has never been indifferent to films about Bolívar. As early as 1938, when Warner Brothers decided to make a film about his life, President López Contreras expressed that

> attention should not be neglected to the laudable purpose of translating accurately the name and prestige of one of the greatest men that humanity has given... Otherwise, it would be to give room for success at the expense of the glories of homelands.
>
> (Izaguirre, 1993: 70)

For his part, Julio Ramos felt that some warnings were needed: "Yes, beware! Be very careful to turn Bolívar, by a deliberate propagandist intention, into a small hackneyed coin because of clumsy hands" (Izaguirre, 1993: 71).

Film critic Luis Álvarez Marcano also collaborated in the discussion by making perhaps one of the clearest claims about the person of the Liberator as "impossible character" by saying that

> Bolívar is unique, he is great, incomparable and there are lives like Christ's that cannot stand the indiscretion of the cinematic camera. Lives that vigorously resist their transfer to the world of cinema as if unconsciously defending their essence thus preventing the possibility of a contradictory or different result from the one sought.

(Izaguirre, 1993: 72)

This thought was shared by Caracciolo Parra Pérez, the most important diplomat of the time.

In his wonderful essay "La accidentada vida de Simón Bolívar por los laberintos del cine" Rodolfo Izaguirre states that

> this excessive and extra cinematic burden of opinion, interventions, warnings, sacralizations, protections, jealousy, anathema and impossibility has affected each one of the film projects which, because of their nonsense or the burden of so many impediments ended up falling apart, sunk into a heavy sea of oblivion.

(Izaguirre, 1993: 73)

This has not prevented filmmakers from representing the Liberator and until today there have been seven feature films whose protagonist is Simón Bolívar: *Simón Bolívar* (Contreras Torres, 1947) starring Julián Soler; the epic film *Bolívar*, directed in 1969 by Alessandro Blasetti and starring Maximilian Schell; *Bolívar, tropikal symphony* directed in 1979 by Diego Rísquez Torres and starring Henrique Vera-Villanueva; *Bolívar soy yo!* directed in 2002 by Jorge Alí Triana; the animated film *Bolívar, the hero* directed in 2003 by Guillermo Rincón with the voice of Manuel Cabral as Bolívar; *Bolívar, the man of difficulties* directed in 2013 by Luis Alberto Lamata Torres and starring Roque Valero; and finally *The Libertator* directed in 2013 by Alberto Arvelo Torres and starring Edgar Ramírez. There are also three films in which Bolívar appears as a secondary character: *The Saint of the Sword* (film about the life of Saint Martin) directed in 1970 by Leopoldo Torre with

12 *Arturo Serrano*

Hector Alterio in the role of Bolívar; *Manuela Sáenz* directed in 2000 by Diego Rísquez with Mariano Álvarez in the role of Bolívar; and finally *Miranda Returns* directed in 2007 by Luis Alberto Lamata with Héctor Palma in the role of Bolívar.

It would be difficult to deal with all the films and the interesting trajectory of this character through world cinema, but let's touch upon at least one of the aforementioned films: the first feature film ever made about Bolívar's life. In my view, this film is the best example of the impossibility of representing Bolívar in film when compared to, for example, representing him in painting (Figure 1.1).

When it comes to representing heroes, painting has a great advantage which comes from the fact that it captures a flash of time. That is, the frozen moment that occurs by stopping time to capture a particular instant. Painting has an advantage because when we think of heroes, we think of them as performing great deeds in specific moments: this or that battle, this or that meeting. If, for example, we think of Bolívar as a hero, a painter can easily create the image of an instant which can easily stand for Bolívar's heroism. The painter can choose the moment that best represents the majesty of the hero. But in cinema things get more complicated, because it doesn't work with moments, but with what Deleuze calls "mobile cuts"[2] (Deleuze, 1997: 2). So, when a filmmaker approaches a subject (character) with awe and shows only the heroic moments, the result is a cardboard character that will never seem real. This is what ended up happening to the film *Simón Bolívar* (Contreras Torres, 1942).

As soon as the film began to be exhibited, there was a curious phenomenon in which the deified figure of Bolívar seemed to be confused with the character of the film. This is the reason why the exaggerated epithets dedicated to the real Bolívar were used to

Year	Film	Director	Screenwriter	Performer	Country
1942	Simón Bolívar	Miguel Contreras Torres	Miguel Contreras Torres	Julián Soler	Mexico
1969	La epopeya de Bolívar	Alessandro Blasetti	José Luis Dibildos	Maximilian Schell	Spain, Italy, Venezuela
1970	El Santo de la espada	Leopoldo Torre Nilsson	Beatriz Guido et alii	Héctor Alterio	Argentina
1979	Bolívar, sinfonía tropikal	Diego Rísquez	Gastón Barbu, Diego Rísquez	Henrique Vera-Villanueva	Venezuela
2000	Manuela Sáenz	Diego Rísquez	Leonardo Padrón	Mariano Álvarez	Venezuela
2002	¡Bolívar soy yo!	José Alí Triana	Miguel Arias, Alberto Quiroga, José Alí Triana	Robinson Díaz	Colombia, France
2003	Bolívar: el héroe	Guillermo Rincón	Ricardo Pachón	(voice) Manuel Cabral	Colombia
2007	Miranda regresa	Luis Alberto Lamata	Henry Herrera, Angélica Vaulla	Héctor Palma	Venezuela, Cuba
2013	Bolívar, el hombre de las dificultades	Luis Alberto Lamata	Luis Alberto Lamata, José Antonio Varela	Roque Valero	Venezuela
2013	Libertador	Alberto Arvelo	Timothy J. Sexton	Édgar Ramírez	Venezuela, Spain

Figure 1.1 Feature films that include portrayals of Simón Bolívar.

refer to the film. The *Mi Film* magazine described the film as "the greatest of our language," and described Julián Soler's representation as the "most plausible than can be imagined" and added that, "this film portrays a grandiose and epic parade of the men who forged our nationality, their virtues, their civility and of their sacrifice" (Tirado, 1987: 95). Both Contreras Torres (director) and Julián Soler (the actor who represented Bolívar) were awarded the highest civic honors by President Medina Angarita of Venezuela in a solemn ceremony.

But soon after, the film began to be seen in a new fairer light. Emilio García Riera wrote in his monumental work of 18 volumes containing more than 6,000 pages, *Historia documental del cine mexicano*, that this film was "a soporific, very long succession of solemn historical gestures embodied by actors, well aware of the transcendentality of their actions and terrified at the prospect of wrinkling the uniforms of the time" (García Riera, 1970).

It is easy to see from García Riera's claims and the opinion of the first critics that the director fell in the trap of the character as a great hero, thus trying to represent the unrepresentable. By losing its sincerity it was impossible for Bolívar, the character, to seem real and therefore the film was destined to fail as a biographic piece. By turning Bolívar's life into a series of great moments, Contreras Torres turned Bolívar into a wax figure.

Cinema is movement and movement is characterized dynamism, action, and change. Good times and bad moments of greatness and lowness, of kindness and evil. They must all be there when they purport to represent the life of a human. Not doing so is to violently manipulate the character to turn him into something rigid and devoid of dynamism and reality. As long as Bolívar was taken as the cult object to which Carrera Damas refers, he would certainly be an impossible character. Bolívar would thus be an impossible citizen not only of Venezuela, but also of the cinematic world.

Contreras' *Simón Bolívar* is, as we have said, the first of many attempts to portray Bolívar in the movies. Each of these attempts presented different problems to their filmmakers. Many of these problems were related to how delicate it is to handle a figure for which Venezuelans feel adoration. But of all those films, it is undoubtedly the films made in 2013 and 2014 that present us the best possibility of understanding the complexities of making, distributing, and exhibiting a film during chavismo.

Using Deleuze's metaphor, we can say that both films have roots that intertwine in the same rhizome. They are not two trees in opposing streets which roots never touch, but rather two bushes that share the same floor, therefore making it impossible to tell their roots apart.

The two Bolívars (2013–14)

The context

Years 2012 and 2013 were very complicated years for Venezuela (Sagarzazu, 2014). Since Chávez was in power in 1999, Venezuelans became more and more polarized. The events of these two very important years will only deepen the contradictions between Venezuelans, thus augmenting the confrontational environment. To properly understand the political mood of the arrival of these films, we have to go back to July 1 of 2011 when Hugo Chávez announced to the nation that he had been diagnosed with cancer and was traveling to Cuba to undertake the necessary treatment. After many trips to and from Cuba, Chávez announced in October 2011 that he was free of cancer. In February 2012, Chávez went back to Cuba for further operations. A debilitated Chávez took part in the Presidential elections and won on October 7. A month later, Chávez returned to Cuba and on December 8, 2012, Chávez announced that the cancer was back, and he needed further treatment. He returned on February 18 only to die a fortnight later. National elections were called and Nicolás Maduro, who had been named by Chávez as his successor, won on April 14 by a very slight margin.

Now it is not difficult to imagine that when these two films arrived, one only three months after Maduro's election and the other one year after, the table was served for a very tense relationship between the films. According to the Venezuelan historian Tomás Straka, almost all films about Bolívar show "the relations between memory and power, the differences between memory as a social phenomenon and historical consciousness as a more academic construction. Also important is the role media can play in this" (Straka, 2014) (Figure 1.2).

In polarized societies function what Howard Gardner calls "the Star Wars plot" (Gardner, 1995). This is a very simple and thus attractive plot used by everybody as children to understand and organize the world.

2012		2013			
October 7th	November 27th	January 10th	February 18th	March 5th	April 14th
Presidential elections	Hugo Chávez announces to the	Presidential Inauguration	Chávez returns to	Hugo Chávez dies	Presidential Elections
Chávez (55%) vs Capriles (44%)	nation that he has to travel to Cuba for further treatment for his cancer	President Chávez didn't since he was still in Cuba.	Caracas in the middle of the night.		Maduro (51%) vs Capriles (49%)

Figure 1.2 Timeline of 2013 events.

This plot remains with us forever as a useful tool to also understand the world. In it, two forces are opposed to each other and everything is interpreted as a part of this larger struggle between good and evil. There is no middle ground. You either belong to my group (good) or you don't (bad). And for a long time, polarization has been the daily bread of Venezuelans. As Robert Samet says, "political antagonism between supporters and opponents of former president Hugo Chávez has been a defining feature of daily life in Caracas for more than a decade" (Samet, 2013).

This is the reason why it shouldn't be a surprise that in a context like the one we have mentioned, which happened in an already highly politicized environment,

> the first film (*Bolívar, el hombre de las dificultades*) was seen as the 'Chavista film' and, based in these criteria shared by many spectators, the other (*The Liberator*) was expected to be, and thus it was as such received, as a more balanced view, almost as the opposite of Lamata's film.
>
> (Straka, 2014)

But is this so? Perhaps we should ask what makes a film Chavista. One of the most commonly mentioned facts of the movie was that it had been financed by Villa del Cine. This institution was founded in 2006 by Hugo Chávez himself with the purpose of "creating the framework necessary to transform Venezuelan film production into an industry" (Macarro, 2018: 57). But the truth was that Villa del Cine never

> ...got rid of the halo of being the political instrument at the service of Chavismo. For this reason, it is not surprising that there were devastating and direct criticisms referring to specific aspects such as the fact that subsidies and funds for the realization of projects were directly related to the ideological and thematic criteria of the regime. Regardless of the implementation of a public contest in an apparently open and transparent process of access to financing, it suffices to look at the titles and content of the products to clearly see that financial aid... is totally linked to the political ideology of the regime.
>
> (Macarro, 2018: 58)

Bolívar, el hombre de las dificultades was, thus, linked from the beginning to Chavismo. This means that if what Macarro (2018) says is true, then we would have to assume that this was a Chavista film. But let's look at two other aspects to see if things are as clear as they seem to be: the plot and the distribution-exhibition process.

The plot

Of all the elements that could be analyzed to ascertain whether a film could be said to correspond to the view Chavismo has of Bolívar or rather to the view the opposition has of him, I will highlight the following two: whether Bolívar is portrayed as a great hero or not and whether the films mention Chávez's hypothesis that Bolívar had been poisoned.

From all that we have been saying up to this moment, it is clear that the first element that should help us in assessing if a film is Chavista or not is whether it places Bolívar in the same place as in the founding documents of Chavismo: that is, in the center. Also, he should be portrayed as the great larger-than-life hero who freed Venezuela. And finally, the most memorable and heroic moments of his life should be shown in an almost pyrotechnic display. In a way, one could imagine a film like Miguel Contreras' being the most appropriate model to make a film that matched the inflamed rhetoric which usually characterized Hugo Chávez discourse on Bolívar. Like the discourse he gave in 2007 to the National Assembly in which he said that "it is necessary to pay tribute every day to Father Bolívar, to 'Our Father who is on earth, in the water and the air' as Pablo Neruda said in his song" (Chávez, 2007).

The second element to be looked for in a film about Simón Bolívar that corresponded to the "ideological and thematic criteria of the regime" (to use Macarro's terms) was the fact that "he –Chávez – claimed Bolívar was the victim of a murderous conspiracy and had been poisoned by Colombian oligarchs. And he wanted forensic scientists to prove it" (Philips and López, 2011).

So, what stories do these movies tell? Lamata himself described *Bolívar, el hombre de las dificultades* in these terms: "this is the story of the 'Bolívar de a pie', poor, exiled, put in doubt." He is not someone who says "This is me. Bolívar. I am the boss." He still has to earn his leadership. He is not an unbeaten hero, he knows defeat. But he has a great virtue: he knows how to get up. He is not a superhero. He is an extraordinary human being (Patria Grande, 2013).

Arvelo, however, confesses to always having wanted to make a film about Bolívar.

> It always seemed to me that Bolívar was an enormously cinematic figure, like a great romantic hero, the person who gives everything

for an idea, for a dream. And I have always been struck by the visuality of the whole phenomenon of Latin American independence: those battles in the mountains, in the jungles, on the plains, it seemed to me that there was an enormous visual force in all this.

(García, 2015)

It is obvious that while Lamata aspired to show Bolívar's human side by making a small biopic about a problematic point in his life, Arvelo planned to be more traditional and show the great hero. Arvelo's reasons are undeniable: the cinematic nature of Bolívar's endeavors in the sense of them being ideal for the big screen. And the budgets reflected this: while Arvelo's film cost 50 million dollars, Lamata's cost was significantly less at one million seven hundred thousand (Llabanero, 2013). While Arvelo's film shows the battles and great moments making unashamed use of the big budget he had, Lamata's film only mentions them at the end of the film in only four lines.

This makes Straka (2014) say that

> very anti-Chavista ladies can applaud what Chávez has been saying for fifteen years if it is said by Edgar Ramírez and the film set belongs to a super production. While, on the other hand, the very human Lamata's Bolívar is accused of Chavista only because Maduro said that he liked it, when in reality this version owes more to the writing of Germán Carrera Damas, John Lynch and Francisco Herrera Luque's *Bolívar de carne y hueso* than to this propaganda that portrays him as a "good savage", a kind of Andrew Lloyd Weber's Che Guevara.

(Straka, 2014)

Nicolás Maduro himself agrees with Straka. In a TV appearance in 2014 he said about *The Liberator* that

> this is the most Chavista Bolívar I have ever seen. You know that Chávez rediscovered Bolívar and the thesis he put forward is reflected in this film. It is not a historically speaking accurate Bolívar, because a historian could question some of the scenes. It is more of an epic Bolívar. He is a revolutionary Bolívar.

(Telesur, 2014)

And we can do nothing but agree with Maduro and Straka in that it is the film identified as oppositionist the one that better reflects Chávez's views on Bolívar.

About Bolívar's death, there isn't much to say since the facts are there. Lamata's film simply doesn't mention the cause of his death because it is a film that happens between 1810 and 1815. However, Arvelo's film ends on December 1, 1830. To anyone familiar with the story of Bolívar the image of a very healthy Bolívar barely 14 days before dying of tuberculosis is astonishing, to say the least. This image together with a final caption that reads "The official cause of death was tuberculosis" is the final suggestion that Chávez was indeed right: Bolívar had been assassinated.

I think it is undeniable that any spectator who was given the facts about the two films would have probably thought that *The Liberator* was the official film that represented the Chavista point of view, when in fact it was the much smaller and accurate *Bolívar, el hombre de las dificultades*. What Samet (2013) said about Venezuelan politics seems to be true also of supposedly clearly politically sided cultural products: "Despite their different political orientations, the antagonistic poles of 'Chavismo' and 'the opposition' share striking similarities."

As we said in the beginning this is but one of many examples where the feud between Chavismo and opposition has "contaminated," for lack of a better word, a cultural process like the production, distribution, and exhibition of a film like Lamata's and Arvelo's.

Notes

1 Some of the elements that support the claim that it is indeed an official Chavista film are: (a) the film had been financed by the government through Villa del Cine, the official production company which had been founded by Chávez in 2006; (b) its director and main actor were renowned Chávez supporters; and (c) Maduro himself put pressure in cinemas for it to be exhibited massively in Venezuela even if it didn't have enough public.
2 "Cinema does not give us an image to which movement is added, it immediately gives us a movement-image. It does give us a section, but a **mobile section** and not an immobile section+abstrtact movement."

References

Boulton, A. (1982). *Bolivar's Face*. Caracas: Ediciones Macanao.
Carrera Damas, G. (2003). *El culto a Bolívar*. Caracas: Alfa Ediciones.
Chávez, H. (2007). "Discurso de Orden del presidente Chávez en ocasión de la entrega de la propuesta de Reforma Constitucional en la Asamblea Nacional." https://es.wikisource.org/wiki/Discurso_de_orden_del_Presidente_Ch%C3%A1vez_en_ocasi%C3%B3n_de_la_entrega_de_la_propuesta_de_Reforma_Constitucional_en_la_Asamblea_Nacional.
Chávez, H. (2015). *The Blue Book*. Caracas: MINCI.

Chumaceiro, I. (2003). "El discurso de Hugo Chávez: Bolívar como estrategia para dividir a los venezolanos" in: *Boletín de linguïstica*, Vol. 20, August–December, 22–42.
Deleuze, G. (1997) *Cinema 1. The Movement Image*. Minneapolis: University of Minnesota Press.
García Riera, E. (1970). *Historia Documental del Cine Mexicano*. Mexico: ERA Editions.
Gardner, H. (1995). *Leading Minds. An Anatomy of Leadership*. Basic Books.
Izaguirre, R. (1993). "La accidentada vida de Simón Bolívar por los laberintos del cine" In Izaguirre, Rodolfo. *Acechos de la imaginación*. Caracas: Monte Ávila Editores.
Llabanero, N. L. (2013). "Conozca las dos películas de Bolívar por estrenarse: Libertador y El Hombre de las Dificultades." https://albaciudad.org/2013/07/conozca-las-dos-peliculas-de-bolivar-por-estrenarse-libertador-y-el-hombre-de-las-dificultades/.
Macarro, J. (2018). "Cine venezolano: Construcción, invención y adaptación de la *Historia Patria*." *Fuera de Campo*, Vol. 2, no. 3: 54–68.
Patria Grande. (2013). "Entrevista a Luis Alberto Lamata." https://www.aporrea.org/actualidad/n236544.html.
Philips, T. and López, V. (2011). "Hugo Chávez Claims Simón Bolívar Was Murdered Not Backed by Science." https://www.theguardian.com/world/2011/jul/26/hugo-chavez-liberation-hero-murdered.
Report on the 3D facial reconstruction of the Liberator Simón Bolívar. (2010). http://www.simonbolivar.gob.ve/rostro#.U3O404Fl6jM.
Sagarzazu, I. (2014). "Venezuela 2013: un país a dos mitades." *Revista de ciencia política*, Vol. 34, no. 1, 315–328.
Samet, R. (2013). "The Photographer's Body: Populism, Polarization, and the Uses of Victimhood in Venezuela." *American Ethnologist*, Vol. 40, no. 3, 525–539.
Straka, T. (2014). "Bolívar, dos películas, ¿una epopeya?" https://historico.prodavinci.com/2014/07/28/artes/bolivar-dos-peliculas-una-epopeya-por-tomas-straka.
Tirado, R. (1987). *Memoria y notas del cine venezolano 1897–1959*. Caracas: Fundación Newmann.
Vinogradoff, L. (2010). "Chávez se muere por los huesos de Simón Bolívar." ABS. https://www.abc.es/internacional/abci-chavez-muere-huesos-simon-bolivar-201001100300-1132967824215_noticia.html.

2 Short-form documentaries, cyber activism, and resistance by Venezuelan filmmakers

Concepción Cascajosa-Virino and Bárbara Barrios Barreto

Abstract

In recent years, the crisis in Venezuela has greatly restricted the development of its film industry (one of the main cultural areas within the Bolivarian project). With their careers paralyzed by funding problems, many emerging Venezuelan filmmakers have been forced into exile or have found alternative ways to create and distribute their work. In a process of increasingly violent social confrontation, some of these creators have chosen to become politically involved and take sides in the protest movements against the government of Nicolás Maduro. Two of them, Carlos Caridad Montero and Hernán Jabés, have explored the short-film format and social media to share their political views with national and international audiences. In this chapter, we will analyze the projects these directors created in 2017 as a result of the protests against Nicolás Maduro's government. First, we will focus on the documentary series *Selfiementary*, a multiplatform project of 17 videos by Carlos Caridad Montero. Second, we will examine the work of Hernán Jabes, which comprises "Somos más" and the accompanying pieces "Somos todo / Somos todos," "Somos Libres," "¿Qué somos?," and "¿Dónde está la revolución?" created with his daughter Marcela Jabes. Their short-form documentaries, uploaded on YouTube, are useful to assess how Venezuelan directors have adopted cyber activism at a critical juncture: the transformation of traditional film practices and the migration to social media in search of new spaces to express the messages and points of view opposed to the Maduro regime.

Video activism and opposition filmmaking

In recent years, video activism has come to occupy a prominent place among anti-government popular revolts around the world, showing a new form of expression for revolutionary filmic practices. The "cyberactivism 2.0" – based on the use of YouTube, Facebook, and Twitter – "allows regular participation without time or place restrictions and increases the different levels of participation and engagement, allowing an individual to support the protest with a simple link to the other" (Sandoval-Almazana & Gil-Garcia, 2014, p. 368). Creating films, videos, or new media content allows an individual to take "power into one's hand, to challenge entrenched hierarchies and powerful economic and cultural forces" (Marcus, 2016, p. 192) as new software has made producing and disseminating media increasingly simple and cheap (Hight, 2014). Over the years, different subgenres of videos for social media platforms have been developed: mobilization videos, witness videos, documentation videos, archived radical videos, and political mashups (Askanius, 2013, pp. 5–8). Priority has been given to short-form videos, which can be consumed and shared quickly and easily. In this sense, YouTube, which hosts short-duration videos and provides great ease of access, has become a privileged space for video activism because the platform fulfills the necessities for successful video activism, including the social networking aspect that is considered a key driving force toward that success (Cheng et al., 2008). The popularization of mobile devices and social media has redefined organized protests, in which video activism has played a growing role, as the 2010–13 Arab Spring exemplified. In the case of Syria, Wessels (2017) analyzed the work of the young Syrian anti-regime protesters who began recording and uploading their videos on YouTube as new "Kinoks," in reference to Dziga Vertov's Soviet filmmaking collective that sought to bridge social revolution with realist cinematic practice. But video activism has been equally active in Latin America, with significant experiences in countries such as Mexico (Hinegardner, 2011), Chile (Pena et al., 2015), and Brazil (de Sousa & Cervi, 2017). The case of Venezuela is especially noteworthy because anti-government video activism was facilitated by the recent development of Venezuelan cinema.

During the early years of the Hugo Chávez administration, cinema became one of the cultural priorities for the state through the National Film Platform, which allowed a boom in film production and international circulation (Farrell, 2016) as part of a broader strategy to use cultural practices to implement a "revolution of conscience" (Muñoz, 2008). The Chávez administration focused on promoting national cinema by creating another Fundación Villa del Cine (Cinema City Foundation), parallel to the already existing National Autonomous Cinematography Center. Through the new organization, significant capital investment was made to fight Hollywood film narratives and revalue the national cinema so that its projects would be historically conscious and reflect the Venezuelan people (Fuentes, 2015). Villa del Cine dynamized the media production of the country funding projects in genres such as short films, feature films, television series, and telenovelas. Documentaries organized into series with specific topics – such as "resistance," "city," "simple people," "people's communities," and "social and political struggles" (Liberatoscioli, 2017, p. 34) – gained momentum as part of an ambitious plan. In its early years, Villa del Cine served as a collaborating entity to carry out projects by both new and veteran filmmakers. However, the selection of projects aligned with the government's system (Alvaray, 2013), so the films were associated with the revolutionary ideal. Filmmakers were given resources to create with independence from traditional producers, but gradually, the filmmakers were increasingly becoming more dependent on the state. This dependence was particularly evident after Villa del Cine was ascribed to the Ministry of the People's Power for Communication and Information in 2014. The film policy was clearly related to the ambition of the Venezuelan government to play a leading role in the cultural strategy of the Latin American region. The ALBA Audiovisual Production Plan, managed from La Villa del Cine, was an example of this (Villazana, 2013, p. 189).

However, the totalitarian tendencies of the government, exacerbated after Nicolás Maduro came to power, strained relations between the state and many of Venezuela's most prominent filmmakers, who used their cinema to narrate the gradual degeneration of the "Bolivarian Revolution." Venezuelan cinema has been resilient, creating stories that reflect social moments, such as the contemporary fiction films *Pelo Malo* (*Bad Hair*, 2013) by Mariana Rondón or *La Familia* (*The Family*, 2017) by Gustavo Rondón. The traditional interest in the representation of violence and urban poverty by Venezuelan cinema (Arenas de Meneses et al., 2012) served as a favorable framework for an intensive exploration of the severity of the economic and political crisis. For several decades, documentary film has been essential in the history of Venezuelan cinema to express popular discontent and serve as a portrait of the nation. As examples, *Pozo muerto* (1968) by Carlos Rebolledo, *La ciudad que nos ve* (1966) by Jesús Enrique Guédez, and *Araya* (1959) by Margot Benacerraf are part of a key stage of Venezuelan cinema history. Since the 1960s, national documentary filmmakers have reflected through their narratives that Venezuela is an unpredictable country (Ruffinelli, 2005). The non-fiction form has achieved special prominence as a tool for political confrontation since the 2002 coup d'état, where the emergence of new media helped to "expand the theatre of the political documentary" (Couret, 2013). Building off that, the catastrophic economic situation of Venezuela has recently been the topic of many documentaries. Margarita Cadenas' *Femmes du chaos vénézuélien* (*Women of Venezuelan Chaos*, 2017), for instance, follows the daily lives of five Venezuelan women from different backgrounds and generations as they survive the chaos, while Tuki Jencquel's *Está todo bien* (*Everything Is OK*, 2018) deals with the collapse of the public health system. Both films are good examples of traditional exhibition practices and are mostly focused on reaching the international audiences who can access them via the film festival circuit and television channels. But other filmmakers have opted for taking advantage of digital media and using new platforms so that their critical views can reach a wider audience (Calvo de Castro, 2019).

The 2017 Civil Resistance Campaign was a privileged space for an alternative film practice. This practice was favored by a context where networked communications had become one of the main spaces of struggle. In the face of the government's campaign of disinformation and online harassment, participants in the civil resistance movement built their own channels for disseminating information and calling for demonstrations: "Decreasing informational uncertainty under censorship was possible because pro-democratization activists actively engaged in disseminating trustworthy information through their social networks" (Puyosa, 2019, p. 102). Carlos Caridad Montero and Hernán Jabes joined the ranks of activists during the 2017 crisis, using the short-film format and YouTube in different ways to intervene in filmic terms in the situation, as we will examine in the next two sections.

Selfiementary by Carlos Caridad Montero

Carlos Caridad Montero (born in 1967) trained as a filmmaker at the respected International School of Cinema and Television at San Antonio de los Baños in Cuba. Screenwriter, director, and journalist, he quickly gained relevance with the award-winning short films *La estrategia del azar* (1996), *Tarde de machos* (2002), and *Nocturno* (2003). Like many Venezuelan filmmakers, Caridad has combined documentary and fiction in his career. *Maracaibo con vista al lago* (*Maracaibo Overlooking the Lake*, 2007) was his debut medium length-film documentary, while *Bloques* (*Blocks*, 2008), co-directed with Alfredo Hueck, was one of the very few horror films financed by Villa del Cine.[1] Although Caridad Montero's solo debut, the satire *3 Bellezas* (*3 Beauties*, 2014), was a box-office success, he has struggled to finance new projects amid the deteriorating situation of the country. In any case, it is difficult to get bored in Venezuela, as he expressed in the first short documentary of his series "Aburrimiento y Autoritarismo. Selfiementary #1: crisis del billete de BsF. 100 (22-12-2016)" ("Boredom and Authoritarianism.

Selfiementary #1: crisis of the 100 BsF. banknote (22-12-2016)").[2] Indeed, political, social, and economic tensions keep citizens in a constant state of alert. The documentary short-film series *Selfiementary* captures that reality by employing a journal-like format that follows the 2017 protests. The filmmaker felt a call to action: "When the protests begin, the dictatorship takes a definite turn, the parliament becomes unrecognized. There, I said I had to go out to the streets and the form is going to dictate the moment."[3] Then, the documentary works, as Ruffinelli (2005, p. 289) would call it in the 1960s, as "a weapon" used by the director to share his point of view of the contemporary moment. Carlos Caridad Montero defines the first piece of the *Selfiementary* series as a "short visual essay" that arose from Maduro government's measure to remove the 100 *bolivares* note (the highest currency of the country). The government's decision created a sense of chaos that inspired the creator. Accordingly, this first short film is presented as a photograph of what the country was going through. The image of Caracas produces calm, tranquility, a reflective voice, and a dynamic montage. City traffic and endless queues are presented as allegories of a country that is always waiting for something to happen. In less than eight minutes, the director shows us a surreal context: panic in the street and shots of beauty contests on television – images that within their subjectivity resonate like an echo of anguish.

During the 17 audiovisual pieces that make up the series *Selfiementary*, the repetition of individual elements is clear.[4] The director made the documentary short film essentially serve as an observation in the first person; this approach works as a kind of diary of a country in crisis. Caridad uses the self-portrait, or *selfie*, in order to place the audience in the context of the protest throughout the series. Further, the filmmaker works the pieces of the series with a digital camera and an external microphone. Only in the first short film does he use material recorded with his mobile phone, but he applies the use of an application that allows him to use the device's camera as if it were a professional camera. He also uses a handheld camera to create a sensation of closeness to an uncomfortable situation, producing an emotion of uncertainty. Additionally, he combines the use of a medium and a medium-long shot to observe with respect and reflect the fatigue of a population. The camera is always in motion, which makes the audience feel like part of the moment. Moreover, the director reminds the audience of war photography as he runs away from the repression by the government.

Ultimately, the short films denote the director's interest in recording the historical moment in which his country finds itself – using the format not only as a form of political expression but also as a document for memory. His effective use of editing with cuts brings freshness to his work that helps the audience digest the sharp images produced. Music in most of the pieces also adds a touch of modernity to the work. However, the use of musical pieces is not constant throughout the series – for example, the director in pieces such as "Protesta nocturna por los caídos. Selfiementary #17. Caracas, 17 de mayo de 2017" ("Nocturnal protest for the fallen. Selfiementary #17. Caracas May 17, 2017")[5] detaches from this rhythm, replacing it with a subtlety fitting of those who feel respect for what they witness. Another aspect that we feel is necessary to highlight is the use of diegetic music throughout the documentary. In pieces like "La marcha del Primero de Mayo fue acorralada. Selfiementary # 10: Crisis en Venezuela" ("The First of May March Was Cornered. Selfiementary # 10: Crisis in Venezuela"),[6] Carlos Caridad Montero shows a scenario where the demonstrators sing the lyrics of the national anthem, such as "la ley respetando la virtud del honor" ("the law respecting the virtue of honor") in dissonance with the actions of those who repress the demonstrators. The use of the national anthem as diegetic music is repeated in other pieces.[7] Likewise, the author cuts into precise verses of the hymn that are directly questioning the establishment.

Moreover, the director repeatedly shows moments such as a citizen holding the national flag, as opposed to the military holding a rifle. Also impressive is the selection of signs with denunciations held by the demonstrators – such as "He visto a la policía matar a gente inocente, y he visto gente no inocente ser presidente" ("I have seen police killing innocent people, and I have seen not innocent people being president") or "#nomasviolenciaVenezuela" ("#nomoreviolenceVenezuela") – as a way to show the discontent of the people. In this way, *Selfiementary* creates a realist portrait of contemporary Venezuelan society as conflicted as the country itself. On the one hand, despite having a political position opposed to the Maduro government, the director also clearly disagrees with the opposition leaders. On the other hand, Carlos Caridad Montero, as he portrays himself in the videos, is trying to understand and participate in the reality of his country's society. On this, he perceives his work as "a cinema of constant change and evolution. For me cinema is a tool for the knowledge and understanding of reality."

The series *Somos más* by Hernán Jabes: reclaiming the country

Hernán Jabes (born in 1969) studied filmmaking at the Institute of Cinema Training Cotrain in Caracas and founded different production companies to develop his creative works. He won many national and international awards with his short films *900 pánico* (*900 Panic*, 2003) and *La librería* (*The Bookshop*, 2007). His first fiction feature film, the social drama *Macuro, la fuerza de un pueblo* (*Macuro, the Power of People*, 2008), was financed by Villa del Cine, which also supported the project during the writing stage. Jabes' second feature film – the thriller *Piedra, papel, tijera* (*Rock, Paper, Scissors*, 2012) – was both a critical and a box-office success. The film was selected to represent Venezuela at the Foreign Language Film competition of the Academy Awards. Notably, Hernán Jabes actually left Venezuela and settled in Mexico to carry on a successful career as an advertising director and camera operator, earning numerous accolades for his work. When he returned to Venezuela, it was to join the protest against the government, a process he documented in the short films "Somos más" ("We Are More"),[8] "Somos todo / Somos todos" ("We Are Everything /We Are Everybody"),[9] "Somos libres" ("We Are Free"),[10] "¿Qué somos?" ("What Are We?"),[11] and "¿Dónde está la revolución?" ("Where Is the Revolution?").[12] With the films, Jabes forms an audiovisual manifesto that expresses his point of view. Importantly, in the case of these short films, only the last two display material shot by professional-quality digital cameras. The first three were recorded with the director's mobile phone during the protests. Inspired by the impetus and commitment reflected in the work done by Caridad, Jabes decided to start his own project.[13] The filmmaker reflects on his decision to film the protest:

> I wondered: what can I do to try to help in some way? What do I know? It is communicating; it's sharing; it is storytelling; let's try to do things like that. It does not come from a need to grow my career or win prizes. It stems from a need for a citizen to contribute to a genuine and legitimate protest.

Jabes does not hide that his intention in the short-film documentaries was to criticize Nicolás Maduro's government: "I was always aware of what my common thread was, and what my intention and motive were: to protest against a dictatorship-." For the director, the short film was the perfect format for narrating situations such as the Venezuelan one; although explaining the depth and dimensions of the country's current crisis requires more than a feature film, the short film functions as a denunciation. According to Jabes, the short film can create emotion and be direct with the message, which is why it is also perfect for social media. The director gave priority to content: recording the protests and, after their visualization, creating the script for the editing process.

Jabes begins the first short film in the series, "Somos más," by introducing the city of Caracas through its characteristic hills attributed to the most vulnerable population, while a funeral car appears as a harbinger of the result that the repression will have in the coming days of protest. We observe full shots with graffiti writings "SOMOS MÁS" ("WE ARE MORE") and "NARCO PRESIDENTE" ("NARC PRESIDENT") within the slow rhythm of the montage. The camera staggers during that opening scene, as the country does, as a girl holds herself so as not to fall, representing the young people the audience will see. The montage allows viewers to contemplate the protests while the director consistently shares his position. In addition, Jabes uses the song "Tonada de Luna Llena" performed by Natalia Lafourcade and Gustavo Guerrero. It is an original composition by Simón Díaz, one of Venezuela's most influential musicians. This musical piece that is usually embraced by Venezuelan popular culture accompanies the images of young people walking with flags in their hands, expressing themselves during the protest while a helicopter flies in a gray sky over them.

"Somos todo / Somos todos" is the best-rounded piece among the five short documentary films. The piece condensed the point of view of the director, the style, and the story that characterized the full project. The use of the telephone camera gives the pieces a hand-crafted touch, which makes viewers think they are in front of material produced in another era. Although the filmmaker using this device helped him to go unnoticed, it gives the discourse an added value in the critical sense. In other words, by making people feel that they are in another era, the director shows the irony of this type of repression taking place in 2017. The stanza from Ángel Cabrera's song "What Have They Done to Liberty, That I Do Not Know You?"[14] accompanies one of the most direct moments of the short film. The song plays alongside a full shot where viewers can see the military and police assaulting a demonstrator. We can also highlight the fourth short film, "¿Qué somos." It shows a montage that contrasts the figure of the Minister of Defence practicing shots with the images of the protest. People were demonstrating while police were repressing the people and government helicopters were intimidating them. These images were accompanied by a mixture of voices of relevant people from the government and the opposition. Very different in its aesthetic approach is "¿Dónde está la revolución?" which Jabes created alongside his daughter Marcela. In this film, they use footage (some of it shot by other filmmakers) from various parts of the country. Caracas, a modern and chaotic city, protests, while in the country that moves, beauty and poverty coexist. Notably, this short film is a piece that denotes a particular pessimistic discourse for the Venezuelan future, although some optimism appears at the end. However, despite that optimism, it is not easy for Jabes to watch these short films and reflect on the Venezuelan crisis ("It's very disappointing for me to watch these shorts, it makes me sad") as he feels that the bad situation of the country persists.

Conclusion

Carlos Caridad Montero and Hernán Jabes belong to a generation of Venezuelan filmmakers who benefitted from the opportunities granted to young creators by the Bolivarian regimen. Both were among the many who received key financing from Villa del Cine to direct their feature-length debuts in 2008, yet they retained a critical view of the regime. Years later, they went back to their roots in short films. But this time, instead of making the rounds of the film circuit, the videos were used as part of cyber activism. Caridad Montero makes a portrait of Venezuelan society, showing the surrealism lived in the country, while Jabes records manifestations and the contrasting sides of the country. The filmmakers have taken advantage of the new dynamics of communication offered by the internet. They have found in the online platform, and specifically on YouTube, a channel in which they can insert their message. It is space that could not be found within the Venezuelan media. With the benefits offered by the language of the documentary short-film format, the specificities of the Venezuelan social context were made visible.

According to both directors, their work generated a positive response from the audience. Carlos Caridad Montero received comments indicating that *Selfiementary* had been essential to documenting the historical moment that took place in the country, although for his next pieces he hopes for "a specific platform, a newspaper that wants to buy it, a television channel, no longer within my channel, because you need to have a security floor." For film director Hernán Jabes, the feedback for his short films within the country was positive, but they have been used both in European countries and in the United States in activities to denounce the situation of the country.[15] Collectively, the work of these two directors comes arguably close to the principles of the New Latin American Cinema (López, 1988): a cinema born out of mostly impossible conditions and the filmmaker's love, as an act of faith. Further, their work offers a cinema that, although it encountered obstacles (such as censorship), could find new distribution channels. Along these lines, the short-form documentaries from both directors were created under unfavorable conditions and lacked traditional spaces for diffusion but have encountered in YouTube a platform for their dissident voices to reflect.

Acknowledgments

We would like to thank filmmakers Carlos Caridad Montero and Hernán Jabes for giving us their time for interviews during October and November 2019.

Notes

1. A full review of the films produced by Villa del Cine during the period 2006–10 can found in Nieto González (2014).
2. Carlos Caridad Montero. (2017, April 28). *Aburrimiento y Autoritarismo. Selfiementary #1: crisis del billete de BsF. 100 (22-12-2016)* [Video]. YouTube. https://www.youtube.com/watch?v=4KOtUCqGhbw.
3. The interview with Carlos Caridad Montero took place on October 2, 2019 (Skype). All quotes attributed to Caridad Montero, unless otherwise noted, belong to that interview.
4. Caridad Montero shot many pieces that are still unpublished; some of them are in post-production. That is the reason that, although 17 pieces are on YouTube, the total number of pieces rises to #29, and the dates of publication are not chronological.
5. Carlos Caridad Montero. (2017, May 19). *Protesta nocturna por los caídos. Selfiementary #17. Caracas, 17 de mayo de 2017* [Video]. YouTube. https://www.youtube.com/watch?v=eysBx30ZI6c.
6. Carlos Caridad Montero. (2017, May 2). *La marcha del Primero de Mayo fue acorralada. Selfiementary # 10: Crisis en Venezuela* [Video]. YouTube. https://www.youtube.com/watch?v=BT7u9gIpE8g.
7. Carlos Caridad Montero. (2017, May 17). *Marcha de los Músicos en Caracas. Selfiementary #13. 7-5-17* [Video]. YouTube. https://www.youtube.com/watch?v=p8fZzFSAYiQ.
8. Hernán Jabes. (2017, May 8). *Somos más* [Video]. YouTube. https://www.youtube.com/watch?v=kTAQy9JVzEI.
9. Hernán Jabes. (2017, May 9). *Somos todo / Somos todos* [Video]. YouTube. https://www.youtube.com/watch?v=pRK7hE413KE.
10. Hernán Jabes. (2017, July 19). *Somos libres* [Video]. YouTube. https://www.youtube.com/watch?v=5Oe-57rrpIY.
11. Hernán Jabes. (2017, July 31). *¿Qué somos?* [Video]. YouTube. https://www.youtube.com/watch?v=00FE37nIBuQ.
12. Hernán Jabes. (2017, August 26). *¿Dónde está la revolución?* [Video]. YouTube. https://www.youtube.com/watch?v=SFVm3n8uOh0.
13. The interview with Hernán Jabes took place in November 2019 (Skype). All the quotes attributed to Jabes, unless otherwise noted, belong to that interview.
14. Original version in Spanish "Qué te han hecho Libertad, que no te conozco"; the lyric forms part of the song "Qué te han hecho Libertad"

by Venezuelan musician Ángel Cabrera. The song was also created in the context of the protest of 2017.

15 An example is Peña, Rolando [@rolandoart_work]. (2017, June 20). *Lectura del poema "Yo te nombro, Libertad" de Paul Éluard y el video "Somos Todos" de Hernan Jabes, sábado 24 de junio, 7pm #VenezuelaLibre* [Tweet]. Twitter. https://twitter.com/rolandoart_work/status/877111135895420928.

References

Alvaray, L. (2013). Claiming the past: Venezuelan historical films and public politics. *Cultural Dynamics*, 25(3), 291–306. doi:10.1177/0921374013499703

Arenas de Meneses, G., Rodríguez, O., & Delgado Flores, C. (2012). El revés de una mirada rota: cambios en el modo de construcción de la representación social de la violencia a partir del relato cinematográfico venezolano contemporáneo. *Comunicación: estudios venezolanos de comunicación*, 157, 82–92. http://gumilla.org/biblioteca/bases/biblo/texto/COM2012157_82-92.pdf

Askanius, T. (2013). Online video activism and political mash-up genres. *JOMEC Journal*, 4, 1–17. doi:10.18573/j.2013.10257

Calvo de Castro, P. (2019). Cine documental latinoamericano. Conclusiones con base en un estudio transversal con enfoque contextual y formal de 100 películas documentales. *Kepes*, 16, 125–51. doi:10.17151/kepes.2019.16.20.6

Cheng, X., Liu, J., & Dale, C. (2008). Characteristics and potentials of YouTube: A measurement study. In E. M. Noam & L. M. Pupillo (Eds.), *Peer-to-peer video. The economics, policy, and culture of today's new mass medium* (pp. 205–17). Springer.

Couret, N. (2013). The revolution was (over)televised: Reconstructing the Venezuelan media coup of 11 April 2002. *Social Identities: Journal for the Study of Race, Nation and Culture*, 19(3–4), 501–12. doi:10.1080/13504630. 2013.774134

De Sousa, A. L. N., & Cervi, L. (2017). Video activism in the Brazilian protests: Genres, narratives and political participation. *Northern Lights: Film & Media Studies Yearbook*, 15(1), 69–88. doi:10.1386/nl.15.1.69_1

Farrell, M. L. (2016). A close-up on national Venezuelan film support during the Chávez years: Between revolution and continuity. *The Latin Americanist*, 60(3), 371–390. doi:10.1111/tla.12084

Fuentes Bajo, M. D. (2015). El régimen chavista y el cine venezolano. In Ó. Lapeña Marchena & M. D. Pérez Murillo (Eds.), *El poder a través de la representación fílmica* (pp. 137–44). Université Paris-Sud.

Hight, C. (2014). Shoot, edit, share: Cultural software and user-generated documentary practice. In K. Nash, C. Hight, & C. Summerhayes (Eds.), *New documentary ecologies. Emerging platforms, practices and discourses* (pp. 219–36). Palgrave Macmillan.

Hinegardner, L. (2011). "We made that film; there is no filmmaker": La otra campaña, autonomy, and citizenship in Mexico. *Taiwan Journal of Democracy*, 7(2), 95–117. http://www.tfd.org.tw/export/sites/tfd/files/publication/journal/dj0702/006.pdf

Liberatoscioli, M. (2017). La Villa del Cine. El retorno del Estado como productor cinematográfico. In A. Escudero Nahón & D. E. González Calderón (Eds.), *Escenarios y desafíos de la comunicación y la cultura en el espacio audiovisual iberoamericano* (pp. 29–39). Universidad Internacional de Andalucía.

López, A. M. (1988). An "other" history: The new Latin America cinema. *Radical History Review*, 41, 93–116. doi:10.1215/01636545-1988-41-93

Marcus, D. (2016). Documentary and video activism. In D. Marcus & S. Kara (Eds.), *Contemporary documentary* (pp. 187–201). Routledge.

Muñoz, B. (2008). The revolution of conscience. *ReVista. Harvard Review of Latin America*, 8(1), 73–76. https://revista.drclas.harvard.edu/book/pdf-16

Nieto González, A. P. (2014). *Estudio cuantitativo de la producción cinematográfica venezolana en largometrajes de ficción durante el periodo 2006–2010* [Degree Final Project, Universidad Central de Venezuela]. http://190.169.30.62/bitstream/123456789/17484/1/Tesis%20completa.pdf

Pena, P., Rodriguez, R., & Saez, C. (2015). Student online video activism and the education movement in Chile. *International Journal of Communication*, 9, 3761–81. https://ijoc.org/index.php/ijoc/article/view/3413/1515

Puyosa, I. (2019). Venezuelan struggle towards democratization: The 2017 civil resistance campaign. In C. Mouly & E. Hernandez Delgado (Eds.), *Civil resistance and violent conflict in Latin America: Mobilizing for rights* (pp. 85–110). Palgrave Macmillan.

Ruffinelli, J. (2005). Documental político en América Latina: Un largo y un corto camino a casa (década de 1990 y comienzos del siglo XXI). In C. Torreiro & J. Cerdán (Eds.), *Documental y vanguardia* (pp. 285–347). Cátedra.

Sandoval-Almazana, R., & Gil-Garcia, J. R. (2014). Towards cyberactivism 2.0? Understanding the use of social media and other information technologies for political activism and social movements. *Government Information Quarterly*, 31(3), 365–78. doi:10.1016/j.giq.2013.10.016

Villazana, L. (2013). The politics of the audiovisual cultural revolution in Latin America and the Caribbean. In T. Muhr (Ed.), *Counter-globalization and socialism in the 21st century. The Bolivarian alliance for the peoples of our America* (pp. 188–202). Routledge.

Wessels, J. (2017). Video activists from Aleppo and Raqqa as modern-day Kinoks? An audiovisual narrative of the Syrian revolution. *Middle East Journal of Culture and Communication*, 10(2–3), 159–74. doi:10.1163/18739865-01002005

3 Asymmetrical information warfare in the Venezuelan contested media spaces

Iria Puyosa

The Venezuelan case offers a rare opportunity to analyze the information warfare promoted by a government in its evolution from illiberal democracy to authoritarian rule. This chapter explores policies and practices deployed by the Venezuelan government between 2009 and 2020 to control online contested spaces. Economic and legal restrictions to internet access began to be adopted by the Chavez government around 2009, while technical censorship became widespread after 2014. Government-sponsored harassment, automated online propaganda, disinformation campaigns, and just-in-time censorship have interfered with online political debate on Venezuelan for more than a decade. Since as early as 2010, Venezuela's government pioneered bots' use to foster trends in Twitter. Information disorder strategies polluting social media around crucial moments of the ongoing Venezuelan conflict are increasingly common after 2013. The major online propaganda strategies used by the Venezuelan government on Twitter are explained in this work. Finally, the chapter focuses on the increasing involvement of foreign actors from Turkey, Spain, and Russia and their coordination with the *Chavismo* trolls' armies to spread propaganda on Twitter after escalating the geopolitical implications of the Venezuelan conflict after 2017.

Introduction

Venezuela paved the way for the backsliding of democracy in Latin America (Corrales, 2020). Chávez's strategies for eroding democracy included "refunding" the nation by convening a constituent assembly, calling for frequent elections to displace the previous elites, and passing discriminatory laws to silence public debate, attack and limit civil society, and harass the opposition (Corrales & Penfold, 2015; Puyosa, 2019). An unbalanced playing field was created to make it difficult for the opposition to compete genuinely. Besides, control of information and media, as well as limitations on civil society organizing, were instrumental in curtailing pluralism and leading toward an increasingly authoritarian regime (Puyosa, 2019).

The second Chávez's term (2006–12) fits into what political scientists label as competitive authoritarianism (Levitsky & Loxton, 2013). At that stage, the Chavez administration used the courts as instruments of political domination while moving toward a hegemonic party model (Corrales & Penfold, 2015; Levitsky & Ziblatt, 2018; Sanchez-Urribarri, 2011). While increasing control over the media was set, civil society activists' criminalization was also underway (Puyosa, 2019; Puyosa & Chaguaceda, 2017). Since 2014, the Maduro administration has evolved toward the consolidation of hegemonic authoritarianism (Alfaro, 2020; Puyosa & Chaguaceda, 2017).

"Communicational hegemony," a neo-authoritarian control model

The neo-authoritarian communication control model arises within hybrids political regimes (Diamond, Plattner & Walker, 2016), as Venezuela was between 2000 and 2012. At the beginning of the Chavez era, communication experts observed that the building blocks of a State-Communicator model were set. The State-Communicator model arose from the need to spread the emerging elite's ideological vision (Bisbal, 2006). The emerging revolutionary elite props up the confrontation with their political adversaries through a "communication war." The communicational hegemony comes to be the advanced phase in such process (Bisbal, Oropeza, Hernández, Urribarri, Cañizalez, Correa, Abreu & Quiñonez, 2009). The term "communication hegemony" began to be used in Venezuela's official statements after the April 2002 coup. Then, a government-run media system and the financing of a "community" media system that was indeed a network of proxy outlets for political propaganda began to expand (Urribarri, 2007). As of 2007, Chávez proclaimed that within the process of building the new Bolivarian hegemony, it was necessary to free Venezuela from mass media. According to Chavez, mass media was associated with both civil society (which was considered a negative link from his military viewpoint) and "the oligarchy" (Chávez, 2007).

Significant milestones of these hegemonic efforts included the nationalization of the telecom company CANTV (2007), the shutting down of the most popular TV channel RCTV (2007), and the closure of 39 radio stations (2009) (Puyosa, 2015). Between 2004 and 2010, legislation that restricts access to information creates safeguards for national security secrets, establishes norms against public officers' vilification, and creates strict libel laws was enacted (Cañizález, 2015; Puyosa, 2019). Among the best examples of this kind of legislation are the Venezuelan 2004 RESORTE law and its 2010 reform, the Law RESORTE-ME that extended restrictions from radio and television to "electronic media." Regulations limiting access to information and free press remind journalists of potentially high costs from critical expression, thereby promoting self-censorship (Cañizález, 2015). Although there were only two jailed journalists during Chavez's 13 years in power, assaults by his sympathizers and verbal attacks against journalists in official speeches were constant (Solis & Sagarzazu, 2020). The punitive legislation trend continued with the most recent Law against the Hatred and for the Peaceful Convivence, unconstitutionally passed in 2018. The Anti-Hatred Law has been widely used during recent years to jail journalists, activists, and regular social media users.

The communicational control model includes the co-opting of private media through mutually beneficial relationships with owners, who often have a symbiotic relationship with political leadership (Becker, 2014). From the political power, funds are directed (through subsidies and advertising guidelines) to sympathetic media, a form of control widely used in Venezuela in the first decade of *Chavismo* (Canelón, 2016). On the contrary, independent or private media faced various forms of intimidation, going through registration and license requirements, controlling the allocation of raw materials such as printing paper, and selective application of tax legislation (Puyosa, 2019). These mechanisms made it possible to force owners to hand over control of the media with a high impact on public opinion to private entities with close ties with Venezuela's ruling leadership between 2009 and 2017 (Corrales, 2015; Puyosa, 2019).

The communicational hegemony consolidated after 2014. Right after Maduro won highly disputed elections by a thin margin, the news channel Globovisión fell under Chavism-friendly businesspeople's control. In the same year, the government forced the sale of several newspapers, including the two with higher readership *Últimas Noticias* and *Noti-Tarde* and the traditionally conservative *El Universal* (Cañizález & Matos-Smith, 2015).

As a direct consequence of the communicational hegemony, the electoral field became highly uneven. During the 2012 presidential campaign, *Chavismo* controlled six of the eight national television stations and approximately half of Venezuela's radio stations. In most rural states, *Chavismo* has a monopoly of information (radio and print, plus the only open television signals available). In the 2012 campaign, Chávez was on national TV and radio mandatory broadcasting for 100 hours. Likewise, all radio and television stations in the country were obliged to broadcast daily ten government messages of 30 seconds each, featuring the incumbent candidate's campaign slogans. Additionally, the government spent about $200 million on advertising on private radio and television stations. In contrast, the opposition only had access to five minutes of airtime a day, at the cost of $102 million. In short, during the 2012 presidential campaign, the Democratic Unity candidate, Henrique Capriles Radonski, was on TV for four minutes for every 96 minutes of Hugo Chávez aired (Puddington, 2017).

Likewise, the communicational hegemony model tries to restrict foreign media diffusion within national borders. Satellite television and the internet often face financial, technological, or legal obstacles to limit their access and, consequently, their impact on public opinion (Puyosa, 2019). In 2005, the Venezuelan government funded its channel for international news diffusion, Telesur (Zweig, 2017; Bisbal, 2006). Telesur has three main functions: bolstering the global leadership and achievements of the Venezuelan regime and its allies, attacking the values of liberal democracy, and exaggerating social problems in the United States, Western Europe, and Latin American countries center or center-right administrations. Telesur favors news from *Chavismo*'s allies, Bolivia, Ecuador, and Cuba, and positive news related to the Colombian non-state armed groups FARC and ELN, as well as news favorable to Russia, Turkey, and Iran (Sousa Matos, 2016; Puyosa, 2019).

The propaganda emphasized aggressions from abroad and characterized opposition politicians and human rights activists as traitors. Dissenting views were invariably subject to incessant attack and ridicule, and dissenters themselves faced a form of personality assassination in which their ideas were twisted to make them appear foolish, radical, unpatriotic, or immoral (Puddington, 2017). Until the 2017 wave of protests, the limited communicational capacities made it difficult for Venezuelan democratic forces to voice their ideas outside the country.

Mijares (2015, 2017) highlights communicational hegemony among the components of the post-Chávez strategy of *Chavismo* to stay in power. Mijares refers to the communicational hegemony as a component of Maduro's "authoritarian resilience, along with the selective isolationism and the reinforcement of ties with authoritarian powers."

Second-generation internet control and technical censorship

The most blatant political control practices over the internet are blackouts, content filtering by keywords, and DNS blocking. Nonetheless, as of 2009, second-generation controls have become generalized. These subtler and more politically sophisticated controls include the following: temporary restriction of connectivity in regions where protests occur, just-in-time blocking of mobile applications, removal of content by ISPs and by website administrators without legal warrants, throttling of connection speed during political unrest, and high costs of connectivity services (Deibert & Rohozinski, 2010).

Hybrid regimes prefer not to use first-generation control mechanisms. Competitive authoritarianism only recurs to technical censorship when facing widespread political unrest, especially if massive protests amplified by social media threaten their stability (Puyosa, 2015). On the contrary, second-generation control mechanisms are often employed under hybrid regimes and competitive authoritarianism.

Chavismo has been developing a sophisticated structure of political control of the internet since 2010 (Puyosa, 2015; Bradshaw & Howard, 2017; Puyosa, 2018; Bradshaw & Howard, 2019), which is congruent with his communicational hegemony model. The adoption of second-generation internet control mechanisms began in Venezuela after the lessons learned from the #IranElection mobilization in mid-2009 (Puyosa, 2015).

In the literature on internet control, a great deal of evidence supports the claim that authoritarian regimes tend to limit internet access infrastructure development and maintenance (Drezner, 2009). Official Venezuelan statistics from the last quarter of 2019 report an internet penetration of 46.6% in households, while 63.8% of the population has limited access through data plans on cell phones. The total number of subscribers has declined since 2017. This decline makes Venezuela a rare case of a country in which internet penetration is decreasing.

Currency controls established during the Chavez administration adversely affected the telecommunications industry's ability to provide maintenance to the connectivity infrastructure and develop a new infrastructure to keep pace with new technological developments and growing demand. In 2020, the average broadband speed is 2.9 Mbps in fixed connections and 1 Mbps in mobile connections. In addition, electricity rationing often prevents users from accessing their internet connection.

Besides, there is evidence of control and securitization practices that do not require technical mechanisms but employ judicial or administrative means such as taxes on internet usage, complicated regulatory requirements for the operation of ISPs, and prison for political expression on social media (Drezner, 2010; Puyosa, 2015). Finally, mass monitoring and surveillance, use of information published online to harass or prosecute political activists, use of automated propaganda, as well as cyberattacks against activists' opponents or "patriotic hacking" are becoming more prevalent (Deibert & Rohozinski, 2010; Drezner, 2010; Puyosa, 2015; Puyosa & Chaguaceda, 2017).

The neo-authoritarian model includes carrying technical attacks against pro-democratization activists, as well as judicialization of online speech. Intercepting journalists and opposition activists' emails were common in 2011 and 2012 when Chavist activists publicly claimed responsibility for "patriotic hacking" actions. The 2018 enactment of the Law against the Hatred introduced prison sentences of up to 20 years for inciting hatred. Ordinary citizens, journalists, and political activists have already been jailed and prosecuted under this law because they criticized government officers on social media.

In 2013, the first government agency with political control over the internet was created, the Strategic Center for Security and Protection of the Homeland (CESPPA by its Spanish initials). In reaction to the 2014 cycle of protests, the use of second-generation control mechanisms became systematic. Just-on-time blocking of URL or mobile applications and the slowdown of internet connections became a common practice, as well as internet shutdowns in places where demonstrations went underway. Likewise, in 2014, the blocking of content for strictly political reasons is observed for the first time in Venezuela, without any legal justification, as a reaction to the massive protest movement.

After the 2014 wave of protests, non-technical controls were adopted, such as routine police reports of citizen activity on the internet and users' imprisonment for political expressions on Twitter. In a high-profile case, in September 2015, opposition politician Leopoldo López was sentenced to nearly 14 years in prison after prosecutors alleged that he incited violence. As primary evidence in the trial against him, prosecutors presented hundreds of tweets and a YouTube video in which the political leader said, "we have to go out to conquer democracy." In that trial, the key prosecution witness was a linguist who analyzed @leopoldolopez timeline to conclude that his Twitter account was used subliminally to summon anti-government unrest. The United Nations regarded Leopoldo López's imprisonment as arbitrary detention. Another high-profile case was the arbitrary detention of journalist and digital rights activist Luis Carlos Díaz, who was targeted as a scapegoat after the national electrical blackout.

Besides, technical censorship is becoming part of the Venezuelan government internet control toolkit in recent years. Since June 2014, the National Commission of Telecommunications (CONATEL) established a routine practice of blocking web pages that published currency exchange rates. Those websites continued to be blocked until 2019, when the Maduro administration started to allow the chaotic dollarization of retail activity. Since 2017, a growing number of digital media sites have been blocked in the country. Twenty-one digital media are currently permanently blocked due to administrative orders issued by the telecommunication regulatory agency's CONATEL to all residential internet providers. Those media outlets have consistently covered serious cases of illicit enrichment in the Maduro administration, or that frequently allow the expression of the pro-democratization forces' leadership. Tactical social media blocks (Twitter, Instagram, Facebook, and YouTube) by the government-run internet service provider, CANTV, are repeated practices every time democratic forces and figures of the so-called Interim Government announce a crucial public statement.

In January 2019, the government almost entirely blocked Wikipedia (Azpúrua, Chirinos, Filastò, Xynou, Basso & Karan, 2019). In 2019 and 2020, more sophisticated technical interference has been implemented, including DNS spoofing of opposition websites set up to organize volunteers for humanitarian aid. Early in 2019, the telecom regulatory agency CONATEL implemented the opposition VoluntariosXVenezuela website's phishing using sophisticated interception techniques and DNS spoofing to drive traffic to a clone website (Azpurua, Guerra & Rivas, 2019). This technical attack has a dual intent to disrupt pro-democratization organizing efforts and capture data to increase surveillance over grassroots activists.

Information warfare in social media contested spaces

The 2019 Global Inventory of Organized Social Media Manipulation places Venezuela among the ten countries in the world where the government has the highest capacity to carry out online disinformation and propaganda operations (Bradshaw & Howard, 2019). Government-sponsored disinformation and automated propaganda have been notorious in the Venezuelan political environment during the last decade (Puyosa, 2015; Puyosa & Chaguaceda, 2017; Urribarri & Díaz, 2018). Venezuela pioneered the use of automated Twitter accounts in Latin America as early as 2010. With the Chávezcadanga Mission launched in April 2010, the Hugo Chávez administration deployed brigades of "cyber activists" to interfere with social media debates. Since then, the Venezuelan authoritarian regime continues to deploy armies of trolls and bots to flood social media platforms with pro-government propaganda, influence online discussions, harass dissidents and spread disinformation (Woolley, 2016; Bradshaw & Howard, 2017; Puyosa, 2018; Zannettou, Caulfield, Setzer, Sirivianos, Stringhini & Blackburn, 2019).

Because the government currently controls almost all mainstream media outlets directly or indirectly, most Venezuelans rely on social media and mobile messaging applications to obtain information on political issues. Therefore, shaping the circulation of information online is paramount in achieving political objectives. The asymmetry of forces in the online contested spaces is notorious. The Maduro administration has high capacity, abundant resources, and a sophisticated strategy developed over a decade. Meanwhile, the pro-democratization forces have low deployment capacity, and their strategic alignment is affected by political differences within their coalition.

A leaked document from the Ministry of the Interior and Justice, "The Bolivarian Revolution's Troll Army," contained detailed information on the *Chavismo* Twitter strategy.[1] The document included guidelines on creating social media accounts, task groups' organizing, and incentives for disseminating propaganda, including cash transfers to activists' electronic wallets.

The cyber-militia was organized following a military structure of troops, squads, battalions, and brigades. Each troop could manage more than 20 accounts and be part of a squad (ten people) with a tactical mission. Troops belong to any of five squads: Pro-Government, Opponents, Neutrals, Distraction, and Fake News. Fake News and Distraction trolls implement a distraction strategy, while the (False) Opponents deploy the strategy of interference and infiltration. The squads were also organized within battalions (100 people) or brigades (500 people) with a strategic mission. A brigade could operate as many as 11,500 social media accounts. During 2018, over 500,000 Twitter accounts were used for propaganda dissemination. This number may amount to 12% of the active Venezuelan Twitter accounts at that moment.

Government cyber-troops have linkages with public administration agencies, including executive ministers for education, health, food, culture, tourism, and housing. Many are government employees whose primary job is not tweeting, but they serve voluntarily as "digital warriors" to plead loyalty to the regime. Nonetheless, there is also evidence of troll factories working for the Venezuelan government for-profit. It is also crucial to highlight social media propaganda activity by the Strategic Integral Defense Regions and the Integral Defense Operational Zone, both operational structures of the National Bolivarian Armed Forces.

A somewhat more sophisticated mode of manipulating the online contested spaces is introducing distractions to overshadow real debates. Twitter accounts deployed for automated distraction share the following characteristics: digital personas using pseudonyms with a multiplatform presence (Twitter, Instagram, and YouTube). These accounts routinely spread political memes, post links to scandalous news (false or authentic), use emotion-provoking images, and ridicule political leadership. They exhibit high tweeting and retweeting frequency patterns similar to those displayed by automated accounts, but they also keep interactions suggesting a real persona.

A third strategy is designed to infiltrate the structure of the opposition networks. A sort of online community gerrymandering aims to divide opposition groups with tactical differences, favoring fragmentation and obstructing unity. The interference and infiltration strategies target the most polarized communities among the different opposition communities. The accounts of false extremist opponents infiltrate these communities. These false extremists interact with real people belonging to opposition communities to gain their trust. Once their influence had been established, they can introduce new viewpoints and divide with incendiary messages (Puyosa, 2018).

The Maduro administration employs for partisan aims, the telecommunications, political intelligence, and national security agencies' technological base. These State capabilities allow monitoring trends, surveillance of communications by political actors, hacking, phishing operations, IP spoofing, tactical or just-in-time blocking of social media platforms, and DNS blocking of opposition websites. Paid personnel from digital communication structures, party activists who act as volunteers, commercial service providers, and state officials develop online communication actions. The official disinformation and propaganda operation agents receive formal training; Venezuela is one of the few cases in the world where a government offers a training curriculum for trolls.

The Chavista brigades on Twitter carry out amplification tasks, misinformation, positioning of opinion matrices, distraction, attack, dirty war, and defense. Activity on Facebook seems less sophisticated, limited to the amplification of official information and false news dissemination through third-party services. On Instagram and official accounts, they maintain digital personas and sock-puppet accounts for the dissemination of memes and disinformation operations. They also have a vast network of official government media, proxy outlets that serve to deploy propaganda and dirty warfare, and friendly private media that help position their narratives, including the international media RT in Spanish and TeleSur.

Daily, public officials and official Party members receive "operations orders" through dedicated channels on WhatsApp and Telegram. These "operations orders" are issued by the Situational Room of the Vice Presidency of the Republic and go through the Secretary of Agitation, Propaganda, and Communication of the United Socialist Party of Venezuela. "Operations orders" contain detailed instructions for the communication actions of the day.

On the contrary, the pro-democratization coalition has limited resources. Its communicational capacity is low. Moreover, the coalition has difficulties in political alignment to define its strategy in the online contestation spaces. Since the coalition took the form of an Interim Government, the four main Venezuelan democratic parties' coalition has maintained a dual strategy. The coalition attempts to develop a government institutional communication, but they also develop denunciation campaigns typical of parliamentary opposition. This dual communication strategy is not congruent with the context of an authoritarian political regime, in which the pro-democratization forces are actually in a situation of resistance.

The pro-democratization forces do not have a technological base comparable to that of the Maduro's administration. Their amplification capabilities are limited since they managed directly just around 2,500 accounts. Efforts to set the public agenda and position opinion trends are unstable. Instagram and Facebook are also used as channels for institutional communication without building identity narratives or counter-propaganda messages.

Pro-democratization activists do not receive formal training in social media conversations, such as the Maduro administration activists. There is an extensive network of opinion leaders who sympathize with the Interim Government but lack guidelines and mechanisms for aligning them with the strategic objectives. The official media of the Interim Government are only used to disseminate official and concise information. There are no formal guidelines to strategically orient relations with independent digital media favorable to the country's re-democratization.

Additionally, online communication spaces are contested by three other groups: a satellite opposition, an opposition that emphasizes its parallel international agenda, and a dissident opposition that broke from *Chavismo*. The satellite opposition – known as the National Dialogue Roundtable parties or "the Little Table" – plays on the limited board assigned to it by the Maduro administration. "The Little Table" has been efficient in establishing an agenda focused on lifting economic sanctions against Maduro's administration instead of the regime change agenda fostered by the rest of the opposition. The Vente party seeks to position itself politically as a liberal right-wing option, wholly differentiated from the pro-democratization coalition's social democratic tendencies. Vente's opinion leaders attack *Chavismo* as a system and emphasize the ideological dimension of the conflict. Their debate threads are often infiltrated and amplified by government trolls who use their divergent approaches to divide pro-democratization forces. Finally, the dissidence of *Chavismo* is a set of factors that have not yet fully aligned with the pro-democratization coalition. Given their Chavista past, dissidents are viewed with distrust by the traditional opposition grassroots.

Venezuela information warfare, a piece in a geopolitical arm-wrestling

In the recent two years, growing evidence of foreign actors' intervention spreading disinformation related to Venezuela is being collected. Foreign state-sponsored propaganda troops are gathering online to support *Chavismo's* hegemony in Venezuela. In the online information warfare arena, Erdogan's AK Trolls (a propaganda arm of the Turkish ruling party, AKP) are among Maduro's most open backers. At the beginning of 2019, when Juan Guaido took oath as Interim President, it was a vast deployment of tweets supporting Maduro coming from high-rank officers from the AKP and amplified by an extensive network of bots. The AKP troll army propelled the hashtag #WeAreMaduro as a global trending topic. There is also network evidence of coordinated Twitter campaigns involving the Catalonian independence movement and Maduro's Embassy in Madrid. The Embassy issued operation orders followed by the independentists, promoting pro-*Chavismo* propaganda for audiences in Spain, such as the January 2019 campaign that used the hashtag #NoEnMiNombre.

In January 2019, Twitter removed 764 operated from Venezuela and 33 accounts more in June 2019; all these accounts were involved in coordinated influence campaigns fostering polarization in the United States. Some of the accounts focused on sharing links to fake news, and others amplified that content through retweets (Alizadeh,

Shapiro, Buntain & Tucker, 2020). The network data analysis reveals that these accounts were linked to the Maduro administration's Ministry of Information and Communication. Interestingly, these Venezuela-based accounts helped spread pro-MAGA content and radical Black Lives Matter messages, apparently intending to contribute to the US Twittersphere's polarization. These Venezuelan accounts were taking part in operations in which Russian and Iranian accounts were also involved.

The US public opinion is one of the most active digital battlegrounds concerning the Venezuelan political conflict. Maduro's Foreign Ministry created the #TrumpHandsOffVenezuela hashtag to rally support activists and propagandists over there, including organizations that have received funds from Caracas since 2004. Additionally, there is evidence of Russian propaganda about Venezuela, concentrated around the 2017's cycle of protests, the May 2018 fraudulent presidential election, and Guaido leadership's January 2019 rise. Russian propaganda directed toward Venezuela reveals a stereotypical vision of "Westernized" political debates. Or maybe just the hasty translation of US polarizing topics into the very different context of Venezuela. Thus, Russian trolls' attempts to use race and morals to polarize Venezuelans are highly ineffectual. Venezuelans had been polarized around the distribution of wealth and progress, not so much about race and religion. Indeed, Venezuelans continued to be polarized nowadays but about the different paths toward regimen change and democracy's recovery.

Note

1 Ministry of the Interior, Justice and Peace (2017). "Ejército de Trolls de la Revolución Bolivariana." Available at https://ipysvenezuela.org/alerta/gobierno-incentiva-la-vigilancia-redes-sociales-la-difusion-noticias-falsas/.

References

Alfaro, F. J. (2020). Archipiélagos políticos bajo la tormenta en Venezuela: Coaliciones, actores y autocratización. *Revista Europea de Estudios Latinoamericanos y del Caribe*, 109, 21–40.

Alizadeh, M., Shapiro, J. N., Buntain, C., & Tucker, J. A. (2020). Content-based features predict social media influence operations. *Science Advances*, 6(30), eabb5824.

Azpúrua, A., Chirinos, M., Filastò, A., Xynou, M., Basso, S., & Karan, K. (January 2019). From the blocking of Wikipedia to social media: Venezuela's political crisis. https://vesinfiltro.com/noticias/report-jan-2019/

Azpúrua, A., Guerra, C., & Rivas, J. L. (January 2019). Phishing by Venezuelan government puts activists and internet users at risk. VE-Sin Filtro. https://vesinfiltro. com/noticias/Phishing_by_Venezuelan_government_targets_activists/

Becker, J. (2014). Russia and the new authoritarians. *Demokratizatsiya*, 22(2), 191.

Bisbal, M. (2006). El Estado-comunicador y su especificidad. *Revista Comunicación*, 134, 60–73.

Bisbal, M., Oropeza, A., Hernández, G., Urribarri, R., Cañizalez, A., Correa, C., Abreu, I., y R. Quiñonez. (2009) *Hegemonía y control comunicacional*. Caracas: Editorial Alfa/UCAB.

Howard, P., & Bradshaw, P. (2017). Troops, trolls and troublemakers: a global inventory of organized social media manipulation. Oxford, Oxford Internet Institute), https://www.oii.ox.ac.uk/blog/troops-trolls-and-troublemakers-a-global-inventory-of-organized-social-media-manipulation/, accessed on August, 14, 2017.

Bradshaw, S., & Howard, P. N. (2019). *The global disinformation order: 2019 global inventory of organised social media manipulation*. Project on Computational Propaganda.

Canelón, A. (2016). El Estado Anunciante 14 años del "mito de gobierno" de Hugo Chávez. En Bisbal, Marcelino, ed. La comunicación bajo asedio: balance de 17 años. Universidad Católica Andrés Bello.

Cañizález, A. (2015). Libertad de prensa y de expresión en los países andinos. Tensión, amenazas y restricciones. Intento de Balance 2013–2014. *Temas de Comunicación*, 29.

Cañizález, A., & Matos-Smith, M. (2015). El caso de Globovisión y la implantación del modelo mixto-autoritario en el sistema de medios. *Iberoamericana*, 15(59), 127–40.

Chávez, H. (2007). Statement by commander President Hugo Chávez at the International Communication Conference "The right to inform and be informed." Presidency of the Republic of Venezuela.

Corrales, J. (2020). Democratic backsliding through electoral irregularities: The case of Venezuela. *European Review of Latin American and Caribbean Studies*, 109, 41–65.

Corrales, J. (2015). The authoritarian resurgence: autocratic legalism in Venezuela. *Journal of Democracy*, 26(2), 37–51.

Corrales, J., & Penfold, M. (2015). *Dragon in the tropics: Venezuela and the legacy of Hugo Chávez*. Washington, DC: Brookings Institution Press.

Deibert, R., & Rohozinski, R. (2010). Liberation vs. control: The future of cyberspace. *Journal of Democracy*, 21(4), 43–57.

Diamond, L., Plattner, M., & Walker, C. eds. (2016). *Authoritarianism goes global: The challenge to democracy*. Baltimore, MD: JHU Press.

Drezner, D. W. (2010). Weighing the scales: The Internet's effect on state-society relations. *The Brown Journal of World Affairs*, 16, 31.

Levitsky, S., & Loxton, J. (2013). Populism and competitive authoritarianism in the Andes. *Democratization*, 20(1), 107–36.

Levitsky, S., & Ziblatt, D. (2018). *How democracies die*. New York: Crown.

Mijares, V. (2015). Venezuela's Post-Chávez foreign policy. *Americas Quarterly*, 9(1), 74.
Mijares, V. (2017). Die Resilienz des venezolanischen Autoritarismus. *GIGA Focus Lateinamerika*, 2.
Puddington, A. (2017). Breaking down democracy: Goals, strategies, and methods of modern authoritarians (pp. 1–2). Washington, DC: Freedom House.
Puyosa, I. (2015). Political control on the Internet in the context of a hybrid regime. Venezuela 2007–2015. *Teknokultura*, 12(3), 501–26.
Puyosa, I. (September 9, 2018). Venezuelan government strategies for information war on Twitter. Available at SSRN: https://ssrn.com/abstract=3459724 or doi:10.2139/ssrn.3459724
Puyosa, I. (2019). Rusia, Venezuela y el ALBA, compartiendo malas prácticas para el control de la información y de la sociedad civil. (Russia, Venezuela and ALBA, sharing bad practices for the control of information and civil society.) In Kozak, G., & Chaguaceda, A. (eds.), *La izquierda como autoritarismo en el siglo XXI*. Buenos Aires: CADAL.
Puyosa, I., & Chaguaceda, A. (2017). Internet control in five political regimes in Latin America. Available at SSRN 3459753
Sanchez- Urribarri, R. (2011). Courts between democracy and hybrid authoritarianism: Evidence from the Venezuelan Supreme Court. *Law & Social Inquiry*, 36(4), 854–84.
Solis, J. A., & Sagarzazu, I. (2020). The media smells like sulfur!!! Leaders and verbal attacks against the fourth estate in unconsolidated democracies. *Political Communication*, 37(1), 20–45.
Sousa Matos, É. (2016). Diplomacia pública y América del Sur. De los conceptos a la práctica: Telesur y el caso venezolano. *Desafíos*, 28(1), 399–426.
Urribarri, R. (2007). Medios comunitarios: el reto de formar (se) para la inclusión. *Comunicación: Estudios venezolanos de comunicación*, 137(1), 45–53.
Urribarri, R., & Díaz, M. (2018). *Políticas públicas para el acceso a internet en Venezuela*. Santiago: Derechos Digitales.
Woolley, S. C. (2016). Automating power: Social bot interference in global politics. First Monday, 21(4). [Online journal available at https://firstmonday.org/ojs/index.php/fm/article/download/6161/5300]
Zannettou, S., Caulfield, T., Setzer, W., Sirivianos, M., Stringhini, G., & Blackburn, J. (June 2019). Who let the trolls out? Towards understanding state-sponsored trolls. In Proceedings of the 10th ACM Conferencse on Web Science (pp. 353–62). ACM.
Zweig, N. (2017). Televising the revolution as cultural policy: Bolivarian state broadcasting as nation-building. *Global Media and Communication*, 13(2), 181–194.

4 Rebellious audiences
Information platform migration and use of WhatsApp in a tyrannized society

Carmen Beatriz Fernández

Abstract

In Venezuela, the populist-authoritarian regime has been creating a new structure for national communications since 2007, where the media scheme favored the official voice. Their goal was consolidated in 2013, when Maduro assumed his presidency after the death of Chavez. After that hegemonic control of media channels, Venezuelan audiences began to migrate to other non-traditional media channels, including digital media, which reached very high numbers. This analysis assesses how audiences have been migrating during the last decade from different information platforms. The migration happened, as a process, in different stages. The chapter also highlights the importance of alternative channels, based, among other sources, on official data from the official opposition TV channel in YouTube and primary data from public opinion polls. The findings suggest that in 2020 WhatsApp is the new destination for Venezuelan audiences seeking political information. This chapter also uses cluster analysis to propose a taxonomy for users of WhatsApp in Venezuela.

Tyrannization: is a neologism needed?

The word "democratization" appeared in 3,257 academic articles in the library index of my university, Universidad de Navarra. I looked then for the opposite term "tyrannization" and it appeared in only three articles, one of them as related to insomnia and two to bullying. But social tyrannizing exists and is a process that leads from democracy to autocracy, and that in Venezuela began at the end of the 20th century with the authoritarian populism of Hugo Chavez. Populism was in Venezuela the transition to tyranny.

In Venezuela the populist regime created a new communicational architecture, in which the new national media scheme clearly favored the official voice. The effort started in 2004, but it was consolidated in 2013, the same year that Chavez passed away. After the hegemonic control of media channels instituted, Venezuelan audiences started to migrate to other non-traditional media channels, including digital media. The aim of this chapter is to evaluate the importance of those alternative channels, based on data from the official opposition TV channel in YouTube, and from other data, including a national poll conducted during January 2020.

Democratization in the late 20th century Huntington suggested an unstoppable global trend. Over 30 countries worldwide shifted from authoritarian to democratic systems of government between 1974 and 1990. Overall, the world saw remarkable processes of democratization and progress for over three decades. There are abundant cases that explain its process (Diamond, Przeworski), which entails a transition from authoritarianism to democracy, the strengthening of fundamental institutions, respect for human rights, the separation of powers, the search for freedom of the press, and the right to information. The tyrannization of societies has been less documented and researched (Norris, P., & Inglehart, R. 2019, Levitsky & Ziblatt 2018). From the 1970s to the end of the 20th century, the number of electoral democracies rose from about 35 to over 100 (Fukuyama, 2015). The number increased dramatically because, after the fall of the Berlin Wall, many societies under the "steel curtain" began a process of democratization. The promise of convergence in the political and the economic realm lived its best times. However, that optimistic notion was just an unfilled promise. Tyrannization matters. In Venezuela it started with populism in 1998. Chavez was a nice "strong man" who felt a special connection with his people, such a strong connection that it did not need any intermediary institution. Few years later, Maduro would attempt to complete the antidemocratic task.

Communicational hegemony

A "communicational hegemony" was the goal of Chávez' government since the Simón Bolívar National Project of 2007, in which the concession of RCTV (the leading private open TV outlet) was withdrawn. The new communicational architecture was set from that point. The new national media scheme favored the official voice. The effort started in 2004 but was consolidated in 2013. The Venezuelan presidential election of April 2013 threw a virtual tie between the two political blocks that made up the country. Henrique Capriles Radonski had competed with Nicolás Maduro, who had been anointed as heir after the death of Hugo Chavez. After Maduro assumed the presidency, efforts to achieve the "communication hegemony" were intensified. Chavismo achieved communicational hegemony almost at the same time that it began to become a political minority, from 49% of popular support in December 2013 to 20% in September 2015 (Datanálisis 2013, 2015). Reaching political balance in the country in 2013, one of the halves was silenced by the media due to the restrictions of the new media system that consolidated the government's communication hegemony.

During the second semester of 2013, a new communicational architecture was consolidated (Fernández, 2018), with a national media scheme that clearly privileged the official voice. From having only one official television signal in 2004, this number grew to six in 2013. The government operated three national radio circuits and more than 250 community radio stations, most of them mere repeaters of the official line. To this were added three newspapers financed with public funds and numerous private media, but with an editorial line aligned to the official one. The consolidation of the hegemonic communication model and the government's control over the media were achieved by combining aggressive media occupation with an effort, facilitated by the government, for friendly businessmen to acquire private media.

Unlike what happened in 2007, when concessions were withdrawn from RCTV, the new model implemented by Maduro was less aggressive than that of his predecessor Chávez: it consisted of buying the media with a neutral or favorable editorial line. The acquisition was not forced and was paid for at high prices, although it is possible that there might have been pressure from the government to sell (Reyes, 2013). In this way, the government of President Maduro managed to obtain a network of media and oligopolistic control of information, aligned in the message with the official voice.

However, a different thing happened with audiences. Even when the media could be bought and sold in the market freely, audiences do not trade their media consumption as easily, and they assumed clearly rebellious positions. A television audience report (Nielsen, 2013) showed that five private television stations were watched by almost half of the national audience, while the group of national public television stations had only 8% of the total viewers. The Venezuelan state failed in its effort to win over audiences. After the revocation of the RCTV concession in 2007, the audience numbers of the successor channel (TVES) decreased significantly: from an average of over 30% to less than 2% (Fernández, 2018).

The failed effort to conquer their own audiences resulted in the indiscriminate use of radio and television networks. President Chávez spoke on the national radio and television network for more than 100 hours a year (Monitoreo Ciudadano). An even more intense pace was followed by his disciple Nicolás Maduro, with an average of half an hour daily, as reported by the monitoring of the NGO Monitoreo Ciudadano (2013–20). With the increase in radio and TV channels, the country's cable operators found a very important incentive for sales of paid channels. The cable television industry in Venezuela grew to such a level that today two thirds of urban households have access to subscription television, free of national channels.

After the design of this new communicational architecture, and the hegemony of the consolidated message during the second half of 2013, the penetration of cable television increased by 11 points, from 55.75% or 1,177,748 homes with the alternative service to open-signal TV, to more than two thirds of the country, 66.86% equivalent to 1,390,608 households (AGB Nielsen, 2013).

After the notorious failure in audience numbers during the Chavez government, the new model of media occupation promised to improve. However, the media controlled since Maduro's presidency also experienced a constant decline in the affections of the audiences. Nielsen's audience measurement of August 2013, after the sale of Globovisión, gave the channel only 3.18%, when it used to be around 8%, doubling that figure in electoral periods.

But not only television audiences migrated to pay TV. There were also internal tropisms in the digital media. Both phenomena agree with what was identified by Iyengar and Hahn (2009): there is growing evidence that in the new media scheme, voters identify biases in the news channels and look for alternative sources of information that are more consistent with their political preferences. The existence of

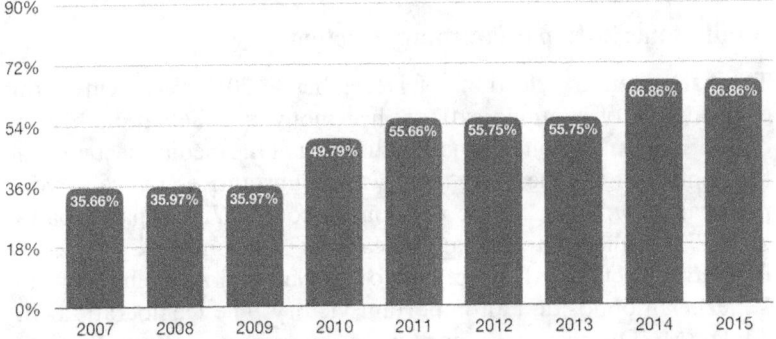

Figure 4.1 Penetration of pay TV in Venezuelan households (2007–2015).
Source: AGB Nielsen Venezuela / LAMAC.

alternative information options makes it possible for audiences to contrast information sources and decide to change channels and/or migrate platforms. The development of cable TV and the existence of numerous informational options on the Internet create a much more fragmented and competitive information environment than one that could have existed 20 years ago, giving audiences wider range to choose sources.

These audience preferences were also shown in news sites on the Internet. During that semester of great changes in the owners of the media and the editorial lines, showing their ideological posture, the ranking changed. The top five digital media sowed the deliberate decision of the audiences of not accompanying the editorial changes. The new media architecture in Venezuela made it easier for the government to control and guide the national news agenda, but this new communicational architecture proved incapable of reversing political opinions and sympathies.

A classical view of media consumption might tell us that it might be determined by the predispositions of the audience, which seeks to confirm or reinforce their opinions in the media content (Lazarsfeld, Berelson and Gaudet, 1972). When analyzing the data of sources to get political information, crossed according to the voter's political preferences, the phenomenon of selective exposure occurs, as pointed out in a previous article (Rodríguez-Virgili and Fernández, 2017). Twenty-six percent of Venezuelan opposition supporters reported social networks as their main means of political information, while only 8% of the ruling party's partisans do the same. That is, citizens seek information that aligns as closely as possible with their previous ideas about reality. Our statistics from YouTube opposition's channel can support the selective exposure theory in the Venezuelan populist case.

A milestone: 2015 parliamentary election

The parliamentary elections of December 6, 2015 were held in this environment of communicational hegemony and the nationalization of information. Despite the nationalization of the media spectrum and the control of the message, there was a substantive change in voter political preferences, in the election outcome. With a participation of 74.17% of the electorate, an increase of 7.7% compared to the 2010 legislative elections, the elections to the National Assembly gave the Venezuelan opposition an important victory. The Democratic Unity Table (MUD), the main opposition movement against President Nicolás Maduro, reached 112 deputies out of the 167 who make up the National Assembly (CITE). With 56.2% of the national vote, the opposition won 72% of the parliamentary representation and closed the long cycle of electoral victories for Chavismo that had lasted 17 years and more than a dozen elections.

At the beginning of the race the campaign and the election ran into an obstacle that seemed difficult to overcome: the government's monopoly on communications. It is within this framework that the YouTube channel was devised as a fundamental platform for the communications of the Democratic Unit. The platform became an alternative to the official voice that reached a peak in its audience levels on election night, after the anxiety of a long delay in the delivery of results.

The YouTube channel reached broad audiences, repeatedly superior to those of open-signal TV channels, and thus became an important informative alternative to that of the official voice. "We had peaks of 90 thousand people watching the live broadcast," says Maria Fernanda Flores, founder and manager of the channel (CITE). Since 2007, Venezuela has been the Latin American country with the most intense use of the network as an instrument of political activism (Fernández, 2008). The cyber-citizen used the network as a prosthesis of freedom: to alleviate their deficiencies, either in their capacity for political action or in their possibilities of obtaining free information, in a society with reduced freedom of the press.

The average user of the channel "Sala de Prensa Unidad" was male (67%), between 25 and 44 years old, and accessing the channel from Venezuela. Already in the statistics of the users it is clear, even at this time, the growing demographic importance of the Venezuelan diaspora, especially the one based in the United States, Colombia, and Spain, and the attention that it gives to local politics. Even to date, the Venezuelan migratory exodus was incipient, and will reach a higher proportion in the following years.

After the parliamentary election, voters were asked, in a nationwide survey, which had been the most used means of communication to inform themselves of the electoral event. By then in Venezuela, TV was still the main medium chosen by ordinary voters to inform themselves politically, with 26% of voters reporting through open-signal TV, with content controlled to a greater or lesser extent by the national government (Datincorp, 2016). However, a similar number (23%) did so through cable channels, or subscription TV, which included high-impact foreign production chains with great interest in local politics, such as CNN, TVE, and Antena 3. The social networks and Internet publications together reached another important 26%.

The data from the citizen political information channels based on the political preferences of the voter, as already pointed out in previous

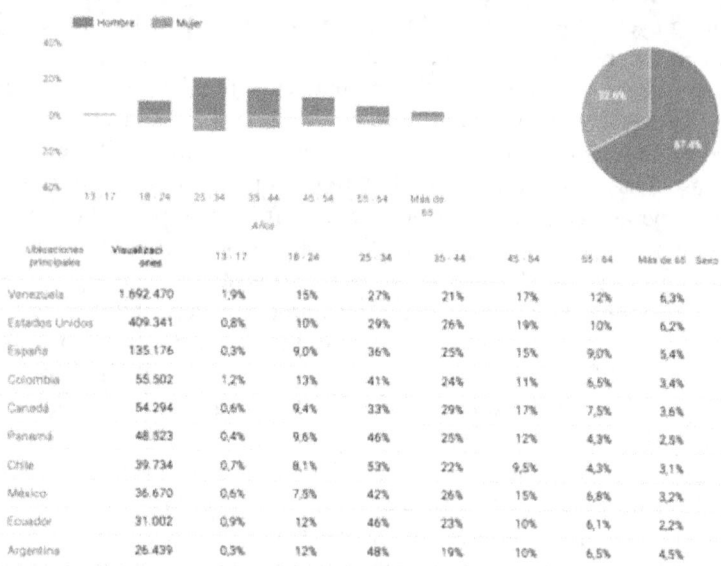

Figure 4.2 Profile of the users of the Unit's press channel on YouTube.
Source: Analytics from the Press Room Unit channel on YouTube.

articles (Rodríguez-Virgili and Fernández, 2017, Serrano-Puche et al., 2020), showed some interesting trends. We found that those TV channels whose editorial management was dominated by the government were used as a means of political information mainly by those who are supporters of the government. While 36% of supporters of the ruling party used open-signal TV as the main political information channel, only 17% of the opposition did the same. Regarding social networks as the main means of political information, the exact opposite was found: 26% of the opponents informed themselves politically through the RRSS, while only 8% of the ruling parties did the same. In total 36% of Venezuelan opponents had their main source of political information from digital (social networks plus informative publications on the Internet), while only 12% of supporters of the ruling party claimed the same.

Also, in social networks citizens seek information as closely aligned as possible with their previous ideas about reality. These results confirm the theory of selective exposure: media consumption is determined by the predispositions of the audience, which seeks to confirm or reinforce their opinions in media content (Lazarsfeld, Berelson and Gaudet, 1972). In other words, citizens look for information as closely as possible with their previous ideas about reality (Stroud, 2010). "The theory predicts that, as a way to minimize dissonance, people look for the information with which they hope to agree" (Iyengar and Hahn, 2009) (Figure 4.3).

For fear of being recipients of ideological propaganda, audiences in Venezuela migrated to all communication platforms. This phenomenon is consistent with other political processes studied in the United States (Iyengar and Hahn, 2009). The demand for news varies with the perception of affinity with news organizations in consumer political preferences In an experimental setting, Iyengar and Hahn found that Republican American voters preferred to read news reports attributed to the Fox news network and avoided CNN and NPR news, while Democrats behaved exactly the opposite: dividing their attention between CNN and NPR, but avoiding Fox news. This self-selection based on party affinity was presented not only in news coverage of

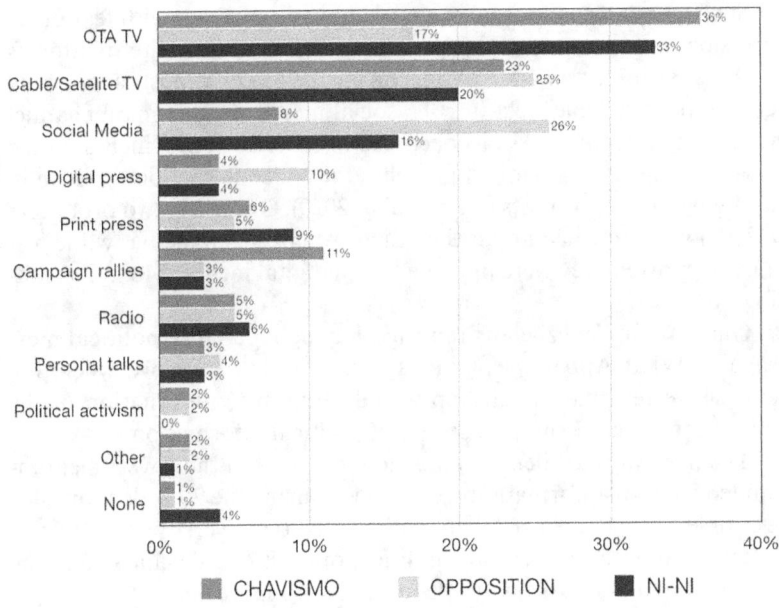

Figure 4.3 Venezuela 2016, platform by political preferences.

Source: Datincorp Venezuela, national survey, with verbatim suggested by Carmen Beatriz Fernández, April 2016, $n = 1,207$.

Question: *During the last parliamentary elections, which channel did you use the most to find out about the electoral process?*

controversial events, but also with respect to relatively innocuous matters such as crime and travel.

The communication hegemony has not been able to prevail over the citizen voice. The media was powerful putting together the agenda of the issues that are discussed in the country ("agenda setting"), but they have been much less effective in changing the opinions of voters and their political behavior.

However, as the Maduro government in Venezuela advanced in the installation of an autocratic project, new ways to silence unofficial voices were designed by the central power, and social networks began to be penetrated and controlled. The new media had offered a window to freedom and diversity of information, but in 2014 the government created a new Vice-Ministry of Communication for Social Networks, with regulatory efforts, while the repression reached social networks. The incarceration of several tweeters was an alert message to this entire community. In 2017, a "Law against Hate" was enacted, which sought to support repression 2.0 that mainly targeted Internet users and distributors of online content and information.

Such government "noise" in social network, together with fear of repression, might have pushed Venezuelan users to use other platforms with less visibility, as WhatsApp. During the heavy protests against the government in Venezuela in 2017, social media was the main channel for getting informed. As has occurred in other societies, including the Arab Spring, social media diminishes the collective action problem in anti-government protests (Hamanaka, 2020). One every two protesters (47.9%) was informed about the rally through social media, while just 15.4% reported they were informed from digital media (More Consulting, May 2017).

One in four Venezuelans reported having received a political message via WhatsApp in the previous week. The data were overwhelming and suggested that WhatsApp would be the new destination in the migration of platforms as a source of political information.

The new ways to silence opposition voices from the government included a few disinformation techniques. During the 2018 elections, for example, the Maduro government impeded the diversity of online expression, to interfere with the political opposition's discourse and the organization of civil society (Puyosa, 2018) (Figure 4.4).

Puyosa identified three different government disinformation strategies on Twitter: coordination of official and automated accounts to ensure reaching the daily trending topics; promotion of distracting hashtags accompanied by emotional, scandalous, misleading,

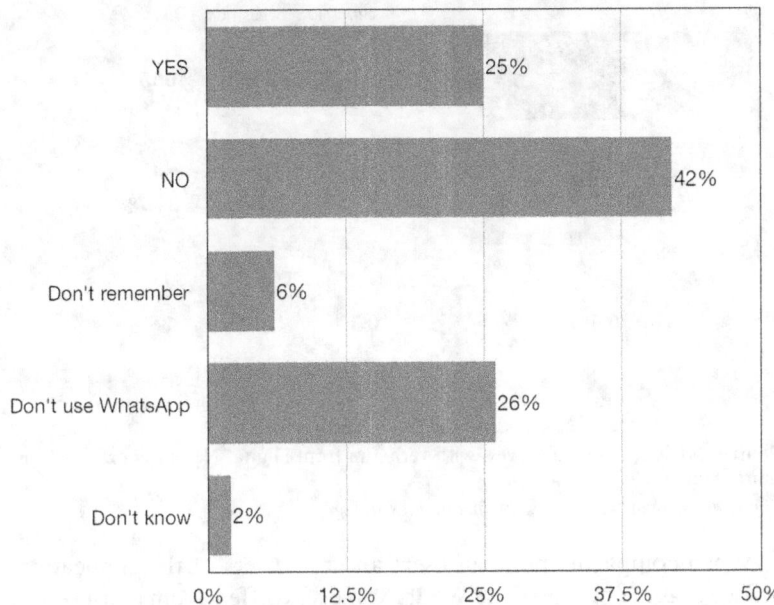

Figure 4.4 Venezuela: Use of WhatsApp for political information, Dec 2017.
Source: Datincorp Venezuela, national survey, with verbatim suggested by Carmen Beatriz Fernández, December 2017, *n* = 1,009.
Question: During the last seven days did you receive any political content by WhatsApp?

offensive, and/or false messages through cyborg and bot accounts; hijacking of oppositional hashtags to distort their messages and interfere in the conversations of the various opposition communities.

Trending: cyber politics 2020 with WhatsApp

Foreseeing a new trope for national audiences, we inquired in a nationwide survey about the role of WhatsApp as a source for political information searching for alternative forms of access to information.

Two out of every three Venezuelans use WhatsApp. However, analyzing among opposition members this number increases to 81.3%, while among chavistas it decreases to 57.2%.

The initial sample was one thousand two hundred and sixteen (1,216) cases. It was refined to analyze only WhatsApp users; thus, the final sample was made up of eight hundred and thirty-four (834) cases (Figure 4.5).

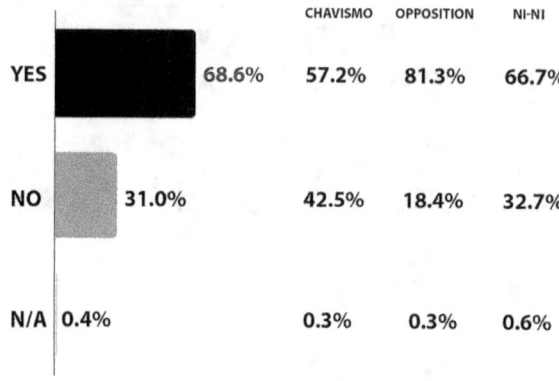

Figure 4.5 Venezuela: Use of WhatsApp, January 2020.
Source: MORE, national survey, with verbatim from Digital News Report questionnaire, January 2020, n = 1,009.
Question: Do you use WhatsApp instant messaging?

When comparing between users and non-users of the application, we see that the profile of the WhatsApp users differs from non-users in the following: (i) age – as age increases the use of WhatsApp decreases; (ii) level of study reached – where the higher the level of study achieved, the greater the use of WhatsApp; (iii) the socio-economic level – where the use of WhatsApp is greater in the upper strata; and (iv) the political self-positioning – where the opposition supporters tend to use the messaging system more than those who support Maduro.

One in three Venezuelans have reported to have heard a voice message with a news and/or rumor via WhatsApp, during the previous week. Also, one in three have read the headlines of the news. One out of every four clicked the links seeking to read the entire notice. One in five forwarded the news and/or a voice note with a rumor.

Cluster analysis was used to create a political taxonomy of the Venezuelan users of WhatsApp. Cluster analysis is a multivariate statistical technique with the purpose of dividing a set of objects into groups so that the profiles of the objects in the same group are very similar to each other (internal cohesion of the group) and those of different cluster objects are different (external isolation of the group). For the analysis, the statistical software Spad version 5.6 was used (Figure 4.6).

The result was obtained from the analysis of several variables from the survey, as were: gender, age, educational level, political self-positioning, interest in news, trust in news, intensity of WhatsApp use.

KNOW-NOTHING (22% of the total WhatsApp users): The main characteristic of this cluster is their total passivity before news reaches

	TOTAL MENTIONED
I saw the headlines, but did not read the news	29,5%
I clicked a link wanting more information for a notice	24,4%
I sent a news article	10,6%
I made RT to a news article	19,5%
I discussed about a notice in a chat group	11,3%
I discussed privately (with one or two people) about a notice	19,4%
I heard a voice note from WhatsApp on a notice/rumor	30,6%
I sent a voice note from WhatsApp on a notice/rumor	18,4%

Figure 4.6 Venezuela: Use of WhatsApp, January 2020.
Source: Data from MORE, national survey, January 2020, $n = 834$.
Question: Regarding the news that comes to you by WhatsApp instant messaging, which of the following have you done last week?

them through WhatsApp. Members of this cluster do not report that they receive news from the platform. They are apathic and disinterested in what is happening in their country and/or in the world. They are mostly young, between 18 and 24 years old. From medium-low socioeconomical level, most of them check their WhatsApp messages just once per day (Figure 4.7).

I DON'T CARE (7%): The main characteristic of this group is their total indifference and distrust for news and politics. They assume that all politicians are equal. In this group the lack of interest is a deliberate attitude. The use of the term "fake news" to discredit politicians did not worry them at all. They are used to give no response when asked about their ideological position. Their political belief is "All politicians are the same."

ALWAYS IN RED (14.5%): The main characteristic of this group is their political position oriented to Chavismo and the Maduro presidency. They identify with the government and consider themselves to be on the extreme left. They use WhatsApp to get news, and receive voice notes from the platform. Their educational level tends to be low (incomplete secondary) as does their social status. They are commonly mature men (45–54) from the urban sectors. Their main source of political information is the TV. They are concerned about disinformation to the extent that foreign agents might be involved. They might be concerned about using the term "fake news" to discredit politicians.

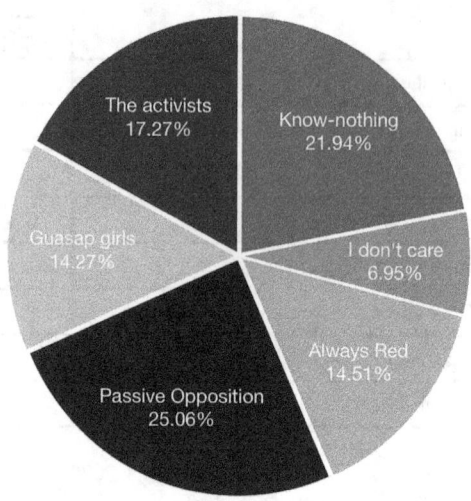

Figure 4.7 Political taxonomy of WhatsApp users, January 2020.
Source: Data from MORE, national survey, January 2020, *n* = 834.

PASSIVE OPPOSITION (25%): This cluster belongs to the upper stratum with completed university studies, and politically center-right opponents. They usually read the headline news through WhatsApp, even when they also get news and information from social networks, and they might discuss the news privately.

GUASAP GIRLS (14%): Members of this group are mostly females. They are active WhatsApp users who might read the headlines, forward the news, or listen to audios. They usually discuss about news privately. Their political position is "All politicians are the same." Their educational level is incomplete secondary. They belong to poor rural social strata, and mainly their news sources come from conversations with family and friends. They are concerned about the citizens and/or members of their community as agents of disinformation.

THE ACTIVISTS (17%): This cluster is the most active in the use of WhatsApp for getting news. They oppose the Maduro regime. They might read news headlines and go to the links to read the entire story. They listen to audios and forward them. They forward the news and discuss them privately. They have a high level of education, completed university or postgraduate, and belong to the upper strata of the population. They can be said to be addicted to the news (receiving them at least twice a day, and most of them six and ten times a day) and seek to interact from it with the rest of the people. They are very concerned about the use of the term "fake news" to discredit politicians.

Discussion

The phenomenon of the increase in the relative importance of new media is global. However, the issue seems to be more intense and accelerated in the Venezuelan case, where, in addition to a migration of audiences from the analog to the digital world, there is a deliberate rebellion and an ambition to escape the control of information from the national government.

This analysis has shown how audiences migrated in successive stages from one platform to another, in a bid tried to find a safe place from tyrannization, in digital platforms.

WhatsApp was the last of these stages, and the newest migratory destination for Venezuelan audiences seeking political information. The cluster analysis identified a political taxonomy for six different types of users of WhatsApp. Each group member is similar to each other, showing their internal cohesion, and different to those members of the other groups (external isolation of the group). From the "know-nothing" (22%) group to the anti-government activists (17%), there is a gradient of different users and uses. The balance is clearly favorable to the anti-government side, which reinforces the importance of WhatsApp platform for the Venezuelan opposition.

When Chavez won his first election in 1998, Venezuela was the oldest democracy in the subregion, and had been leading the democratization of the continent. Venezuela helped decisively the democratization of Central America, Brazil, and the Southern Cone, and its support was equally important in the subregional rejection of the regime of Alberto Fujimori, the penultimate dictatorship of the continent. However, the worst fears with Chávez were fulfilled. During his popular government, and through plebiscitary mechanisms the Venezuelan case marked a negative inflection in the global democratizing era. A democratic setback with 30 years of democratization of the world has been reversed since 1998. What finally will happen with Venezuelan democracy will say whether the tyrannization of a society deserves or not to be the subject of study in the next decade.

References

AGB Nielsen Media Research Venezuela. (2013). *Medición de audiencias*. Agosto. «Medición de audiencias». Caracas: Nielsen.

Datanálisis. (November 2013, 2015). «Encuesta nacional ómnibus». Caracas: Datanálisis.

Datincorp. (April 2016 & December 2017). «Encuesta nacional». Caracas: Datincorp.

Fukuyama, F. (2015). Why is democracy performing so poorly? *Journal of Democracy*, 26(1), 11–20. doi:10.1353/jod.2015.0017

Fernández, C. B. (2008). *Ciberpolítica: ¿cómo usamos las tecnologías digitales en la política latinoamericana?* Buenos Aires: Konrad Adenauer Stiftung.

Fernández, C. B. (2018). Medios rojos y espectadores azules: cuando las audiencias deciden emigrar. Selectividad ideológica de las audiencias ante la estatización de la información en Venezuela. *Contratexto*, (029), 181–198.

Hamanaka, S. (2020). The role of digital media in the 2011 Egyptian revolution. *Democratization*, 27(5), 777–96. doi:10.1080/13510347.2020.1737676

Huntington, S. P. (2000). The clash of civilizations?. In *Culture and politics* (pp. 99–118). Palgrave Macmillan, New York.

IIES-UCAB. (2012). «Entorno comunicacional venezolano: la consolidación de un modelo». Proyecto Monitor Electoral Presidencial 2012. Caracas: Instituto de Investigaciones Económicas y Sociales de la Universidad Católica Andrés Bello.

Iyengar, S., & Hahn, K. S. (2009). Red media, blue media: Evidence of ideological selectivity in media use. *Journal of Communication*, 59(1), 19–39. doi:10.1111/j.1460-2466.2008.01402.x

Lazarsfeld, P. F., Berelson, B., & Gaudet, H. (1972). *The people's choice: How the voter makes up his mind in a presidential campaign*. New York: Columbia U.P.

Levitsky, S., & Ziblatt, D. (2018). *How democracies die*. New York: Crown.

Lijphart, A. (2012). *Patterns of democracy: Government forms and performance in thirty-six countries*. New Haven, CT: Yale University Press.

Monitoreo Ciudadano. (2020). http://monitoreociudadano.org/cadenometro/

Norris, P., & Inglehart, R. (2019). *Cultural backlash: Trump, Brexit, and authoritarian populism*. Cambridge University Press.

Przeworski, A. (2018). *Why bother with elections?* Cambridge, UK: Polity Press.

Puyosa, I. (2018). Venezuelan government strategies for information war on Twitter. *SSRN Electronic Journal*. doi:10.2139/ssrn.3459724

Reyes, L. M. (10 de junio del 2013). La venta de los medios en Venezuela. *Politikom*. Recuperado de http://politikom.wordpress.com/2013/06/10/la-venta-de-los-me- dios-en-venezuela/

Rodríguez-Virgili, J., & Fernández, C. B. (2017). Infopolítica en campañas críticas: el caso de Argentina, España y Venezuela en 2015. *Comunicación y Hombre*, 13, 85–102.

Serrano-Puche, J., Fernández, C. B., & Rodríguez-Virgili, J. (2020, in print). "Disinformation and news consumption in a polarized society: An analysis of the case of Venezuela", in The Politics of Technology in Latin America. Volume 2: Digital Media, Daily Life and Public Engagement. Chapter 11. Routledge Avery Plaw, Barbara Carvalho Gurgel, and David Ramírez Plascencia (Editors).

Stroud, N. J. (2010). Population and Partisan Selective Exposure. *Journal of Communication* 60(3), 556–576. https://doi.org/10.1111/j.1460-2466.2010.01497.x

5 From riches to rags
The decline of Venezuelan telenovelas

Carolina Acosta-Alzuru

Abstract
In 1994, economist Abdel Güerere classified telenovelas as Venezuela's most important non-traditional export and envisioned a prosperous future for this media product. In 1999 the country produced 8–12 telenovelas a year. Today no telenovelas are produced in Venezuela and the country's once powerful telenovela industry is virtually invisible in the international market. This chapter – based on research conducted since 1999 – examines this decline, its causes and consequences. What do these factors say about the relation between the media and government in Venezuela, the country's state of freedom of expression, and the regulation of its discursive spaces in the last 20 years?

Introduction

In 1994, economist Abdel Güerere classified telenovelas as Venezuela's most important non-traditional export and envisioned a prosperous future for this media product (Güerere, 1994). Five years later, when Hugo Chávez became president, the Venezuelan telenovela industry consisted, mainly, of two networks – RCTV and Venevision. Each produced four to six telenovelas per year. Competition between them had defined Venezuelan television since the 1950s. A third network, Televen, filled its programming grid with Brazilian melodramas.

Today Venezuelan telenovelas are virtually invisible in the international market. RCTV is off the air, Venevision has not been producing telenovelas since 2017, and Televen ended a co-production deal with Cadena Tres (Mexico) and Telemundo (USA) that yielded one production in 2013 and another in 2014. Meanwhile, state network TVes broadcasts *Diriliş Ertuğul*, a Turkish drama favored by President Nicolás Maduro (Maduro visits set of Turkish TV series, 2018).

This chapter examines the decline of the Venezuelan telenovela industry, its causes and consequences. What do these tell us about the shape of the telenovela international market? What do these factors say about the relation between media and government in Venezuela, the state of freedom of expression, and the regulation of discursive spaces in the last 20 years?

Theoretical framework and methods

This chapter is the product of research conducted since 1999. My long-time academic engagement with the telenovela genre, the Venezuelan telenovela industry, in particular, and – more recently – Turkish dramas is guided by the cultural studies insight that media, culture, and society are inextricably linked (Hall, 1997). Using the Circuit of Culture (du Gay, Hall, MacKay, & Negus, 1997) as an organizing tool, I have examined melodramatic genres and the sectors that produce them from the multiple perspectives of representation, identity, consumption, production, and regulation. I use a mix of methods that includes textual analysis, repeated in-depth interviews with production and audience members, focus groups with viewers, document analysis, participant observation on sets, locations and production offices, and news coverage analysis.

The Venezuelan telenovela: then and now

The apparent simplicity of the codes of telenovelas cloaks the complexity of their writing, production, reception, and regulation processes. Furthermore, it belies the vastness and variety of the genre's universe. Generally speaking, all telenovelas can be placed in a continuum that has at one extreme the traditional telenovela "*rosa*" and at the other the telenovela called "*de ruptura*."[1]

Telenovelas rosa are high in melodrama and characterized by a central story of heterosexual love. The main couple has to overcome impediments and schemes to achieve happiness together. These protagonists usually belong to different socioeconomic levels; hence, theirs is a story of socioeconomic ascent – a Cinderella story. Characters are Manichean, the beautiful heroine is sweet, virtuous, and naïve, while villains are pure evil (Acosta-Alzuru, 2003).

In contrast, *telenovelas de ruptura* – a general term used for all telenovelas that break with the *rosa* mold – are more *veristas*.[2] They may include social, cultural, and political issues, and their dramatic structure often involves more than one central love story. Characters are nuanced, complex, and, at times, unpredictable. These narrative fictions combine personal and social problems that speak to the audience in terms of a shared reality (Martín-Barbero & Rey, 1999).

By 1999, when Hugo Chávez became president in a landslide election, the Venezuelan telenovela industry's extensive catalog included a diversity of stories that could be placed throughout the *rosa* ↔ *de ruptura* continuum. On the traditional telenovela side, Venezuela was the original production home of Delia Fiallo's Cinderella-story melodramas, such as *Esmeralda* (1970), with its blind, rural, poor female protagonist, baby switch, and Manichean characters.[3]

Venezuela had also produced melodramas set in a different historical time – period pieces – *telenovelas de época*. Stories set in times of dictatorships were particularly successful, as they portrayed repressive regimes, while telling the love stories that characterize the telenovela genre. Two examples stood out: *Estefanía* (1979), which depicted the underground resistance movement to the authoritarian government of Marcos Pérez Jiménez,[4] and *La Dueña* (1984), a *Count of Montecristo* story of betrayal and revenge with a female protagonist wronged during the times of Juan Vicente Gómez.[5] Both telenovelas were successes.

Telenovelas de ruptura, although not as common as their *rosa* counterparts, were also produced in Venezuela. The most emblematic example is *Por estas calles* (1992), an audience phenomenon that aired for almost 27 months. In it, the central love story disappeared as the telenovela became a chronicle of the country's sociopolitical everyday life in a turbulent time period that culminated with the impeachment of President Carlos Andrés Pérez (Espada, 2004; Rivero, 2010).

Venezuelan telenovela exports followed the evolution of the genre in the international market. First, they were regional exports. Second, they were sold in romance languages countries outside Latin America, such as Spain, France, and Italy. Lastly, they reached other regions of the world – Eastern and Northern Europe, Asia, Africa, and the Middle East (Wilkinson, 2003). In 1996, Venevision already exported to 30 markets, earning more than $20 million (Margolis, 1997). Before that year, Coral Pictures, RCTV's international distribution company, had exported dozens of their productions, including *Cristal* and *Kassandra*. *Cristal* (1986) garnered an 80% audience share in Spain, opening up that important market for Venezuelan telenovelas (Shaw & Dennison, 2005). It was a time in which the genre did not show yet changes due to globalization and the need to conquer international markets (Mato, 2002). The main reason for this is that the domestic market was still the most important factor, given that "advertising sales were far more lucrative than international sales revenues" (Havens, 2005).

In sum, by the time Chávez came to power in 1999, RCTV and Venevision had long been established as telenovela production powerhouses, each with a yearly output of four to six telenovelas and with an important presence in the international market. Their programming grid boasted a primetime with three own produced telenovelas and an afternoon block dominated by a mix of imported and domestically produced melodramas. The third network – Televen – did not produce telenovelas, but filled its programming grid with Brazilian *novelas*, garnering significant ratings and shares in the upper socioeconomic levels ABC, but failing to reach classes D and E, which comprised 80% of the population.[6]

Now the situation is quite different. After the government did not renew the broadcasting license of RCTV and confiscated its equipment in 2007 (Romero, 2007), the network ceased to exist as a broadcaster, although it painstakingly produced two more telenovelas before stopping operations.[7]

RCTV's disappearance in 2007 reduced the Venezuelan telenovela industry by 50%. Only Venevision remained as a producer. Its output diminished to only one telenovela per year. These telenovelas were squarely *telenovela rosa* style: *De todas maneras Rosa* (2013), *Corazón Esmeralda* (2014), *Amor Secreto* (2015), *Entre tu amor y mi amor* (2016), and *Para verte major* (2017). In 2018 Venevision stopped making telenovelas altogether, even though the network had completed scripts by several of the authors that were on its payroll.[8]

Forced by law to include at least two Venezuelan productions daily (Venezuela, 2010),[9] Televen made several attempts at producing its own telenovelas and/or broadcasting national productions. First, it teamed with an independent production company headed by RCTV's former VP of Dramatic Productions, José Simón Escalona[10] Second, it co-produced two telenovelas with Cadena Tres (Mexico) and Telemundo (USA),[11] before the agreement was canceled by the international partners due to the difficulties of producing in politically unstable Venezuela (Roa Viana, personal communication, March 20, 2015). Third, it bought and broadcast two telenovelas co-produced by RTI (Colombia) and Televisa (Mexico) that were remakes of Venezuelan melodramas.[12] And even though these productions were done with non-Venezuela money, they passed as Venezuelan because they were shot in the studios of RCTV.[13] Fourth, Televen decided to broadcast old telenovelas bought from the RCTV catalog.

Summarizing, by 1999 Venezuela was producing 8–12 telenovelas per year. And, at any point, its programming grid boasted four to six new domestic telenovelas. Today, the yearly output is zero. Not surprisingly, this situation has an impact in the country's place in the international television market. In contrast to the sizeable catalogs presented by other countries' production companies, the Venezuelan industry can only offer past glories. For instance, at MIPCOM 2015,[14] Venevision's main product was a set of old telenovelas packaged as *"Leyendas*/Legends" of the genre (CisnerosMedia, 2015). This catalog of older productions was rebranded as *"Las Reinas*/The Queens" for the most important content market in the Americas, NATPE-Miami 2020 (Produ, 2020).

From protagonist to extra

The significant weakening and reduction of the Venezuelan telenovela industry is due to causes that are related to: (a) the country's political and economic context, (b) the sometimes erratic decisions of Venezuelan network executives, and (c) the characteristics of a more competitive global market. These factors have rendered the output reduction already described, and telenovelas with stories and production quality that have difficulty competing in the international arena.

Bland storylines and absence of contemporary topics

A legal framework that regulates media content and affords the government the means to punish broadcasters, and an intimidating governmental discourse that elicits self-censorship are the main factors that shaped the stories and topics included in the last Venezuelan telenovelas. These are stories in the traditional *telenovela rosa* mold that eschew any mention of the country's reality and give a superficial treatment, if any, to controversial and/or contemporary topics[15] for the sake of being "safe" from possible government threats and actions.

The *Ley de Responsabilidad Social en Radio y Televisión* (Law of Social Responsibility for Radio and Television, known for its acronym in Spanish as Ley RESORTE) went into effect in January 2005, seven months after Venevision broadcast to high rating telenovela *Cosita Rica*, whose plot mirrored, and editorialized about, the difficult path to the August 2004 recall referendum of President Hugo Chávez (Acosta-Alzuru, 2007). This media content law, denounced by Human Rights Watch as coercive and stifling of freedom of expression (Human Rights Watch, 2003), imposes severe penalties on media outlets that do not comply with content regulations, and includes strict rules regarding telenovelas' language and storylines. From then on, producing and broadcasting telenovelas with political content or political overtones became impossible.

The situation worsened in 2007 when RCTV's broadcast license was not renewed by the government. Not only did the global telenovela industry lose one of its two top Venezuelan players leaving Venevision without the stimulus of competition, but both surviving Venezuela networks – Venevision and Televen – went into survival mode eliminating any content critical of the government. In particular, Venevision enacted self-censorship by editing and censoring its telenovelas far beyond the rules imposed by the media content law (Acosta-Alzuru, 2014).

Self-censorship was also stimulated by the actions of the government's media regulating entity, CONATEL (Comisión Nacional de Telecomunicaciones). After years importing *narconovelas*[16] for their programming grids, Televen and Venevision were "exhorted"[17] by CONATEL to eliminate them (Gómez, 2010).[18] The regulating entity also required Televen to stop the broadcast of humorous Colombian telenovela *Chepe Fortuna* because Hugo Chávez deemed its content to be "disrespectful to Venezuela" (Chavez hails canceling Colombia TV show for its "disrespect" to Venezuela, 2011). These prohibitions translated into important financial losses for the two affected networks that had already paid for these shows. These losses were then reflected in lower production budgets and the concomitant reduction of production output.

The government's intimidating strategies are not limited to the legal framework and CONATEL's actions. The presidential discourse is an important element, too. For example, early in 2014 when beloved telenovela actor Mónica Spear was murdered in an incident that shook Venezuelans and elicited discussion about the country's levels of crime and violence (Moh, 2014), President Nicolás Maduro blamed telenovelas. He accused telenovelas of "inciting violence and hate" and ordered the revision of all television programming, including TV by subscription (Maduro, 2014). Networks, already in survival mode since the closing of RCTV, went into emergency mode. In Televen, the writers of telenovela *Nora* were ordered to cut the total number of episodes from 120 to 76 (Franceschi, 2014). Venevision, which had four writers working on new telenovelas, decided not to produce any of them, but to do a remake of a 1991 telenovela *rosa*. This seemed like a safer and less expensive option than to broadcast a more contemporary story that could attract the attention of a government determined to control television by using telenovelas as a scapegoat for the country's spiraling violence (Cawthorne & García Rawlins, 2014). In his speeches, Maduro singled out writer Leonardo Padrón as "virulent and violent" (VTV, 2014). Padrón is, arguably, the most successful Venezuelan telenovela author of the last 20 years. He is also a well-known opponent of the government. Padrón writes telenovelas *veristas* and was under contract by Venevisión. Since the last time he was on the air in 2011, Padrón had written a telenovela and a series. And even though he wrote them following the network's requirements of not including any elements from the Venezuelan context, these stories never even made it to the pre-production stage (Padrón, personal communication, December 15, 2015). This is the effect of the presidential discourse: a network that has under contract the most successful writer silenced him. Meanwhile the programming grid became increasingly bland and the global market perceived the Venezuelan product as prudish and less contemporary than its international competitors (Farías, interview, October 17, 2014).

Lagging production values

Advertising investment in television dropped dramatically in Venezuela due to the dire economic situation which includes hyperinflation (Venezuela's inflation tumbles to 9,586% in 2019: Central Bank, 2020), a scarcity index of 28%,[19] a murky and convoluted foreign exchange system, and the government expropriation, reduction, or elimination of several key industries (Pons & Orozco, 2014; Wilson, 2014). Venezuelan television networks were in the red. Hence, production budgets were low compared to their competitors in the international market.[20]

Foreign exchange restrictions further complicated the situation (P.G., 2014), making it cumbersome, difficult, and quite expensive to update equipment and train technical personnel. Hence, in 2013, while production companies around the world were producing already in HD and using a substantial number of exterior locations, Venevisión's equipment and personnel were becoming outdated and studio-shot scenes dominated.

Shooting outside television studios became another uphill battle due to a couple of factors. The first one is the country's soaring crime rate. The capital city of Caracas, where most telenovela scenes were produced and shot, had a rate of 119.87 intentional homicide per 100,000 inhabitants, making it the most violent city in the world (CCSPJP, 2016). These crime rates hindered production outside the studios, especially at night. The second factor was the cost of using locations. Privately owned homes, hotels, restaurants, malls, etc., became very costly due to the country's inflation. The owners of these properties charged exaggerated fees for their use as they saw a financial opportunity when they rented their spaces to networks and production companies, which are perceived as wealthy institutions. Government-controlled locations such as streets, parks, airports, and bus and metro stations need special permits to be used. These permits are not only expensive, but their costs vary on a day-to-day basis. The procedure to get the permit also changes frequently. And there were cases in which, after the network paid and acquired the permit, the controlling entity revoked it on the actual production day because one of the actors in the production schedule had been vetoed by the government for expressing her political views. Needless to say, the money paid for the permit was not reimbursed (Fraiz Grijalba, interview, October 22, 2013). These difficulties' end result was that production minimized shooting in exterior locations and this further lowered the production quality of Venezuelan telenovelas in an international market in which telenovela production quality is closing the gap with film production.[21]

Assumptions and choices

After RCTV disappeared from the airwaves, Venevision assumed it had a captive domestic audience in the absence of its traditional competitor. Executives ordered the network's telenovela authors to write stories geared toward the international market, disregarding the Venezuelan viewers. The term "universal telenovela" was repeated endlessly in conversations with all who worked in writing and production. That meant no stories or characters that could be considered "local."[22]

Three years later, on June 24, 2010, for the first time in five decades, there was not a single Venezuelan telenovela on Venezuelan television. In addition to the factors already described, the local product had fallen behind the imported telenovelas that Televen was broadcasting. Venevision was stunned. After years catering only to the upper socio-economic levels by broadcasting Brazilian telenovelas, Televen had discovered the formula to reach all socio-economic strata and compete effectively against sole domestic producer Venevision: broadcast Telemundo telenovelas. Telemundo's melodramas displayed significantly higher production values and told stories that Venevision could not afford on its Venezuelan screen because of the legal/political environment.

Venevision's executives had miscalculated the strength of the audience's attachment to local production when they decided to prioritize international sales, assuming that without RCTV, they owned the domestic market. The audience moved gradually to Televen, as they felt disconnected from the storylines presented by Venevision, and the Telemundo telenovelas offered daring plots and lavish production.

Soon the domestic market became unimportant. Networks privileged legal survival over audience ratings. Broadcasting licenses are "the Sword of Damocles" for Venezuelan networks. It is more important then, not to be scolded, suspended, or canceled, than to be watched. It is the death not only of telenovelas, but also of commercial television as we know it.

It must be noted, however, that network executives still hoped to sell internationally because in days of dismal local advertising investment in the media, exports become crucial to stay afloat. Venevision, in particular, took Mexico's Televisa as its role model, trying to emulate its emphasis on traditional style telenovelas, which are better suited for Venezuela's regulatory context. The network insisted that writers use "neutral" vocabulary and actors speak with a "neutral accent" meant to be more palatable to the same audiences that Televisa caters to. This meant using more Mexican vocabulary and accent. The consequence was that they produced telenovelas that not only did not tell Venezuelan stories but also did not sound Venezuelan. Ironically, this did not help the country's melodramas in the international market either (Orozco Gómez & Vassallo de Lopes, 2013, 2014, 2015).

From riches to rags

The reduced output of Venezuela's telenovela industry and the characteristics of its latter products are the consequences of the factors detailed in the previous pages. In turn, the small number and low quality of those telenovelas have become the main cause for the unimportant place currently occupied by Venezuelan telenovelas in the international market.

To be sure, the telenovela industry is not the only one severely diminished in Venezuela. The country's food, car, and pharmaceutical industries (to name only the most important ones) are barely producing. Shortages are chronic and exports are nil (Lansberg-Rodríguez, 2016; Sivira, 2016; Venezuelan auto industry in free fall amid economic woes, 2014).

But economic context aside, what happened to the telenovela industry is in line with the government's admitted goal of achieving "communication hegemony."[23] The Ley RESORTE, and CONATEL's and the president's intimidation of media outlets work toward that objective. In addition, economic groups related to the government have bought key media outlets such as network Globovision, daily *El Universal*, and media conglomerate Cadena Capriles, which publishes the country's most read newspaper – *Últimas Noticias* (IPYS, 2014; Meza, 2014). Now these outlets rarely include content critical of the government. In particular, the award-winning investigative reporting unit of *Últimas Noticias* was dismantled after the buyout.[24]

Newsprint is controlled by government agency Corporación Maneiro. Important opposition newspapers have had to close because they received no paper (Borrero, 2016; Corporación Maneiro ahorca la libertad de expresión, asegura Jorge Roig, 2015; CPJ, 2016). Over 40 radio stations did not have their licenses renewed by the government in 2015 because of their oppositional stance, while many have turned to self-censorship to avoid the same fate (IPYS, 2015) and in 2017, 40 more radio stations saw government mandated interruptions of their broadcasts (IPYS, 2018). The end result of this list of threats, buyouts, closings, and restrictions is increasing government control of media content and a loss of media freedom.

As Venezuelan telenovelas became less in number and "safer" in content, they disappeared from the programming grids that once they had occupied around the world. More importantly, a discursive space disappeared in Venezuela. That discursive space was a place where Venezuelans were used to seeing their everyday life reflected in stories and characters that spoke directly to them. Venezuelan telenovelas tackled political, economic, and health-related issues (Acosta-Alzuru, 2007, 2010, 2013, 2015). Their reduction and domestication are yet another way of limiting the space for dissent and the representation (and discussion) of topics related to government inefficiency and corruption. It is one more way to control discourse in a country undergoing an unprecedented complex humanitarian and human rights crisis (Amnesty International Report on Venezuela, 2019; UN Human Rights report on Venezuela urges immediate measures to halt and remedy grave rights violations, 2019). In the process the Venezuelan telenovela became a product that did not speak like, or to its domestic audience. But, given its performance in the international market, it is clear it does not speak to non-Venezuelan audiences either.

It is the inverse of the traditional telenovela "Cinderella" plot so prevalent in *telenovelas rosa*. Instead of rags to riches, Venezuelan melodramas have gone from riches to rags. This is not only their story, but also the recent history of a country named Venezuela.

Notes

1 These telenovelas have also been termed as "neo-baroque" (Calabrese, 1989), "stylistically postmodern" (Steimberg, 1997), and "naturalist" and "realist" (Vassallo de Lopes, 2009).
2 *Verismo* was a literary movement that began in Italy in the late 19th century. Its main tenet was that literature should portray society like a photograph, even including its most sordid details.

3 Fiallo, considered *"la reina del culebrón"* (the telenovela queen), wrote many successful telenovelas rosa in the 1960s, 1970s, and 1980s, before retiring and selling the rights of her stories to Mexican network Televisa.
4 Pérez Jiménez ruled Venezuela from 1949 to early 1958. He "forced many former associates into exile and tortured, murdered and incarcerated hundreds of other opponents" (Rohter, 2001).
5 For 27 years (1908–35), Gómez ruled the country. Under him, "Venezuela became a centralized State. The government had control of the national territory and regional caudillos disappeared. The methods of political control were cruelly repressive" (Pérez Perdomo, 2007).
6 Nielsen and other research companies such as Datanálisis classify Venezuela in five socioeconomic levels: A and B are "high" classes, C is the upper middle class, D is the lower middle class, where there are signs of moderate poverty, and E comprises those who live under the poverty line. By 2011 the makeup of the country was 3% A and B, 17% C, 38% D, and 42% E (¿En qué clase social se ubica usted?, 2012).
7 On September 2015, the Inter-American Court of Human Rights ordered the Venezuelan government to reinstate RCTV's broadcasting license (Murillo, 2015). The country's Supreme Court declared this ruling "non-executable" (TSJ declara inejecutable fallo de la CIDH sobre RCTV, 2015).
8 *Malajunta* and *La Casa Cerrada*, by Leonardo Padrón; *Gritos del Corazón*, by Martin Hahn; *Amores Mágicos*, by Doris Segui; *Vivir a Prueba*, by Mónica Montañés and José Manuel Peláez, among others.
9 In particular, note Artículo 7, numeral 3; Artículo 29, numeral 3; and Artículo 35, disposiciones tansitorias primera y segunda (Venezuela, 2010).
10 Épica Producciones produced for Televen *Nacer Contigo* (2012), which did not succeed in the afternoon block.
11 *Dulce Amargo* (2012) and *Nora* (2014).
12 *Las Bandidas* (2013), a remake of *Las Amazonas* (1985), and *La Virgen de la calle* (2013), a remake of *Juana la virgen* (2002).
13 In 2007 when the government did not renew RCTV's broadcasting license, the only thing the government did not confiscate was RCTV's building. The company, then, rented its studios to independently produced shows, such as the Venezuelan version of *Who Wants to Be a Millionaire? (¿Quién quiere ser millonario?)*, and to international telenovela producers.
14 MIPCOM is the largest worldwide annual international convention of entertainment content (MIPCOM).
15 For instance, in *Tomasa Te quiero* (2009), a subplot including a compulsive gambler never showed scenes that included actual gambling.
16 *Narconovelas* are telenovelas with stories set in the drug trafficking world. These are imported from Colombia and Telemundo.
17 "CONATEL exhorts..." is the vocabulary used by the regulating entity. The networks understand this language as a direct order, and they comply without any attempts to respond, state their case, or appeal (Acosta-Alzuru, 2014).
18 Even TV by subscription has been exhorted to eliminate *narconovelas* (Conatel pide a cableras no difundir "narconovelas," 2016).
19 This figure is from January 2014. The Venezuelan Central Bank has not updated the indicators since then (Renwick & Lee, 2015).

20 For example, in 2011 the average cost/episode of a Telemundo telenovela was $70,000, whereas Venevision spent about $20,000–$35,000 per episode (Stopello, personal communication, February 27, 2011). This gap grew wider.
21 For example, Telemundo's *La Reina del Sur* boasted a 90%–10% locations-studio ratio (Stopello, personal communication, February 27, 2011) and Colombia's *Escobar, el patron del mal* was completely shot in 450 exterior locations (Lo que no se supo de 'El patrón del mal,' 2012). Turkish dramas which are dominating the market are shot completely on locations (Acosta-Alzuru, in press).
22 In the interviews I conducted with network executives both in Venezuela and in Miami in the time period 2007–11, the term "local" was defined in a variety of ways. For example, "humor is local, crying is universal," "local is having the characters say *'vale'* in their dialogues," "local is a character allegorical of Chávez," etc.
23 "Socialism requires communication hegemony" declared on January 8, 2007 by then Minister of Information and Communication, Andrés Izarra (Weffer, 2007). In the year 2014, the government's communication budget was 5.37 billion Bolívares, which was larger than the sum of the budgets of 13 ministries (Von Bergen, 2015).
24 The unit received the prestigious Gabriel García Márquez Award from la Fundación para el Nuevo Periodismo Iberoamericano (FNPI) (Unidad de Investigación de Últimas Noticias gana premio Gabriel García Márquez, 2014), and Columbia University's Maria Moors Cabot for their investigation of the February 12, 2014 events where they exposed the responsibility of government security forces in the deaths of two protesters (Past Maria Moors Cabot Prizes Winners, 2020).

References

Acosta-Alzuru, C. (2003). I'm not a feminist I only defend women as human beings: The production, representation and consumption of feminism in a telenovela. *Critical Studies in Media Communication, 20*(3), 269–94.

Acosta-Alzuru, C. (2007). *Venezuela es una Telenovela*. Caracas: Editorial Alfa.

Acosta-Alzuru, C. (2010). Beauty queens, machistas and street children: The production and reception of socio-cultural issues in telenovelas. *International Journal of Cultural Studies, 13*(2), 1–19.

Acosta-Alzuru, C. (2013). Dear Micaela: Studying a telenovela protagonist with asperger's syndrome. *Cultural Studies <-> Critical Methodologies, 13*(2), 125–37.

Acosta-Alzuru, C. (2014). Melodrama, reality and crisis: The government-media relationship in Hugo Chávez's Bolivarian revolution. *International Journal of Cultural Studies, 17*(3), 209–26. doi:10.1177/1367877913488462

Acosta-Alzuru, C. (2015). *Telenovela adentro*. Caracas, Venezuela: Editorial Alfa.

Acosta-Alzuru, C. (in press). Will it travel?: The local vs. global tug-of-war for telenovela and Turkish dizi producers. In Ö. Yolcu, P. Aslan, & C. Mujica

(Eds.), *Transnationalization of Turkish television series*. Istanbul, Turkey: Istanbul University.
Amnesty International Report on Venezuela. (2019). Retrieved from https://www.amnesty.org/en/countries/americas/venezuela/report-venezuela/
Borrero, L. A. (2016, March 17). #17M: La noche más oscura de El Carabobeño. *El Carabobeño*. Retrieved from http://www.el-carabobeno.com/noticias/articulo/121516/17m-la-noche-ms-oscura-de-el-carabobeo
Calabrese, O. (1989). *La era neobarroca (signo e imagen)*. Madrid: Ediciones Cátedra.
Cawthorne, A., & García Rawlins, C. (2014, February 20). Venezuela's violent crime fuels the death business. *Reuters*. Retrieved from https://www.reuters.com/article/us-venezuela-crime/venezuelas-violent-crime-fuels-the-death-business-idUSBREA1J0KM20140220
CCSPJP. (2016). *Caracas, Venezuela, la ciudad más violenta del mundo*. Retrieved from http://www.seguridadjusticiaypaz.org.mx/biblioteca/download/6-prensa/231-caracas-venezuela-the-most-violent-city-in-the-world
Chavez hails canceling Colombia TV show for its "disrespect" to Venezuela. (2011, January 18). *Latin American Herald Tribune*. Retrieved from http://laht.com/article.asp?ArticleId=384091&CategoryId=10717
CisnerosMedia. (2015). Cisneros media distribution presents "Leyendas", a package of classic telenovelas [Press release]. Retrieved from http://www.cisnerosmediadist.com/node/511
Conatel pide a cableras no difundir "narconovelas." (2016, February 16). *El Estímulo*. Retrieved from http://elestimulo.com/blog/conatel-pide-a-cableras-no-difundir-narconovelas/
CorporaciónManeiroahorcalalibertaddeexpresión,aseguraJorgeRoig.(2015,May 29). *El Impulso*. Retrieved from http://www.elimpulso.com/noticias/economia/corporacion-maneiro-ahorca-la-libertad-de-expresion-asegura-jorge-roig
CPJ. (2016). Venezuelan government newsprint squeeze forces newspaper to stop printing. Retrieved from https://cpj.org/2016/03/venezuelan-government-newsprint-squeeze-forces-new/
du Gay, P., Hall, S., MacKay, H., & Negus, K. (1997). *Doing cultural studies: The story of the Sony Walkman*. London: Sage.
¿En qué clase social se ubica usted? (2012, January 16). *El Mundo Economía y Negocios*. Retrieved from http://www.elmundo.com.ve/noticias/finanzas-personales/recomendaciones/%C2%BFen-que-clase-social-se-ubica-usted-.aspx
Espada, C. (2004). *La Telenovela en Venezuela*. Caracas: Fundación Bigott.
Franceschi, K. (2014, May 4). Nora se sobrepone a los obstáculos, pero ya no será emprendedora. *El Nacional*. Retrieved from http://www.el-nacional.com/escenas/Nora-sobrepone-obstaculos-emprendedora_0_401959932.html
Gómez, A. R. (2010, October 30). Censura contra las "narco-novelas." *El Universal*.
Güerere, A. (1994). *Producción de telenovelas*. Caracas: IESA.
Hall, S. (1997). The work of representation. In S. Hall (Ed.), *Representation: Cultural representations and signifying practices* (pp. 13–74). London: Sage.

Havens, T. (2005). Globalization and the generic transformation of telenovelas. In G. R. Edgerton & B. G. Rose (Eds.), *Thinking outside the box: A contemporary television genre reader* (pp. 271–92). Lexington: University Press of Kentucky.

Human Rights Watch. (2003). Retrieved from www.hrw.org/press/2003/06/venezuela062303-ltr.htm

IPYS. (2014). *Caracas: Se concreta la venta del tercer medio de comunicación privado en los últimos 14 meses*. Retrieved from http://ipysvenezuela.org/alerta/caracas-se-concreta-la-venta-del-tercer-medio-de-comunicacion-privado-en-los-ultimos-14-meses/

IPYS. (2015). *La radio de provincia se quedó sin cafeína*. Retrieved from https://www.ipys.org.ve/propietariosdelacensura/radio.html

IPYS. (2018). *Emisoras en vilo*. Retrieved from https://ipysvenezuela.org/emisoras-en-vilo/

Lansberg-Rodríguez, D. (2016, March 11). Getting sick in Venezuela has become a death sentence. *Foreign Policy*. Retrieved from http://foreignpolicy.com/2016/03/11/getting-sick-in-venezuela-has-become-a-death-sentence/

Lo que no se supo de "El patrón del mal." (2012, December 15). *Semana*. Retrieved from http://www.semana.com/gente/articulo/lo-no-supo-el-patron-del-mal/325449-3

Maduro, N. (2014). *Memoria y Cuenta del año 2013*. Retrieved from http://www.slideshare.net/jonbonachon/memoria-y-cuenta-20132014-del-presidente-nicols-maduro-moros?utm_source=slideshow02&utm_medium=ssemail&utm_campaign=share_slideshow

Maduro visits set of Turkish TV series. (2018, July 11). *Hürriyet Daily News*. Retrieved from https://www.hurriyetdailynews.com/maduro-visits-set-of-turkish-tv-series-134444

Margolis, M. (1997). Soaps clean up. *Latin Trade, 5*(4), 46–52

Martín-Barbero, J., & Rey, G. (1999). *Los ejercicios del ver: hegemonía audiovisual y ficción televisiva*. Barcelona: Gedisa.

Mato, D. (2002). Miami in the transnationalization of the telenovela industry: On territoriality and globalization. *Journal of Latin American Cultural Studies, 11*(2), 195–212.

Meza, A. (2014, July 5). La venta de un diario venezolano aviva el debate sobre la propiedad de los medios. *El País*. Retrieved from http://internacional.elpais.com/internacional/2014/07/05/actualidad/1404587135_949473.html

MIPCOM. The World's entertainment content market. Retrieved from http://www.mipcom.com/en/about/

Moh, C. (2014, January 7). Venezuelan ex-beauty queen Monica Spear murdered. *BBC*. Retrieved from http://www.bbc.com/news/world-latin-america-25642041

Murillo, Á. (2015, September 15). La Corte Interamericana condena al Venezuela por el cierre de RCTV. *El País*. Retrieved from http://internacional.elpais.com/internacional/2015/09/08/actualidad/1441667653_119546.html

Orozco Gómez, G., & Vassallo de Lopes, M. I. (2013). *OBITEL 2013: Memoria social y ficción televisiva en países iberoamericanos*. Porto Alegre, Brasil: Globo & Editorial Sulina.

Orozco Gómez, G., & Vassallo de Lopes, M. I. (2014). *OBITEL 2014 Estrategias de producción transmedia en la ficción televisiva*. Porto Alegre, Brasil: Globo & Editora Sulina.

Orozco Gómez, G., & Vassallo de Lopes, M. I. (Eds.). (2015). *OBITEL 2015: Relaciones de género en la ficción televisiva*. Porto Alegre, Brasil: Editora Sulina.

P.G. (2014). A fistful of dollars, or perhaps not: Venezuela's byzantine exchange-rate system. *The Economist*. Retrieved from http://www.economist.com/blogs/americasview/2014/04/venezuelas-byzantine-exchange-rate-system

Past Maria Moors Cabot Prize Winners. (2020). Retrieved from https://journalism.columbia.edu/system/files/content/pastcabotwinnerslist_2.pdf

Pérez Perdomo, R. (2007). Estado y justicia en tiempos de Gómez (Venezuela 1909–1935). *Politeia, 30*(39), 121–50.

Pons, C., & Orozco, J. (2014, February 11). Venezuela planning third dollar supply system as scarcity rises. *Bloombert*. Retrieved from http://www.bloomberg.com/news/2014-02-12/venezuela-planning-third-dollar-supply-system-as-scarcity-rises.html

Produ. (2020). Cisneros Media se plantea crecer en todas las unidades de negocios. *2020 NATPE Miami*, 90–91.

Renwick, D., & Lee, B. (2015). Venezuela's economic fractures. *Council on Foreign Relations*. Retrieved from http://www.cfr.org/economics/venezuelas-economic-fractures/p32853

Rivero, M. (2010). *La rebelión de los náufragos*. Caracas: Editorial Alfa.

Rohter, L. (2001, September 22). Marcos Pérez Jiménez, 87, Venezuela Ruler. *New York Times*. Retrieved from http://www.nytimes.com/2001/09/22/world/marcos-perez-jimenez-87-venezuela-ruler.html

Romero, S. (2007, January 1). Nonrenewal of TV license stokes debate in Venezuela. *The New York Times*. Retrieved from http://www.nytimes.com/2007/01/01/world/americas/01venez.html?_r=0

Shaw, L., & Dennison, S. (2005). *Pop culture Latin America! Media, arts, and lifestyle*. Santa Barbara, CA: ABC-CLIO.

Sivira, R. (2016, January 12). Campo venezolano requiere reactivar su productividad. *El Impulso*. Retrieved from http://www.elimpulso.com/noticias/economia/campo-venezolano-requiere-reactivar-su-productividad

Steimberg, O. (1997). Estilo contemporáneo y desarticulación narrativa. Nuevos presentes, nuevos pasados de la telenovela. In E. Verón & L. Escudero Chauvel (Eds.), *Telenovela: Ficción popular y mutaciones culturales* (pp. 17–28). Barcelona: Gedisa.

TSJ declara inejecutable fallo de la CIDH sobre RCTV. (2015, September 10). *El Universal*. Retrieved from http://www.eluniversal.com/nacional-y-politica/150910/tsj-declara-inejecutable-fallo-de-la-cidh-sobre-rctv

UN Human Rights report on Venezuela urges immediate measures to halt and remedy grave rights violations. (2019). Retrieved from https://www.ohchr.org/EN/NewsEvents/Pages/DisplayNews.aspx?NewsID=24788&LangID=E

Unidad de Investigación de Últimas Noticias gana premio Gabriel García Márquez. (2014, October 1). *La Patilla*. Retrieved from http://www.lapatilla.com/site/2014/10/01/unidad-de-investigacion-de-ultimas-noticias-gana-premio-gabriel-garcia-marquez/

Vassallo de Lopes, M. I. (2009). Telenovela como recurso comunicativo. *MATRIZes, 3*(1), 1–23. Retrieved from https://www.revistas.usp.br/matrizes/article/view/38239

Venezuela, R. B. D. (2010). Ley de responsabilidad social en radio, televisión y medios electrónicos. Retrieved from http://www.scribd.com/doc/45291089/Proyecto-de-Ley-de-Responsabilidad-en-Radio-Television-y-Medios-Electronicos

Venezuela's inflation tumbles to 9,586% in 2019: central bank. (2020, February 4). *Reuters*. Retrieved from https://www.reuters.com/article/us-venezuela-economy/venezuelas-inflation-tumbles-to-9586-in-2019-central-bank-idUSKBN1ZY2YQ

Venezuelan auto industry in free fall amid economic woes. (2014, August 9). *Reuters*. Retrieved from http://www.autonews.com/article/20140809/GLOBAL/140809786/venezuelan-auto-industry-in-free-fall-amid-economic-woes

Von Bergen, F. (2015, May 3). La hegemonía roja. *El Nacional*. Retrieved from http://www.el-nacional.com/siete_dias/hegemonia-roja_0_620937949.html

VTV (Producer). (2014, Enero 26). Maduro contra Padrón. Retrieved from http://youtu.be/5L9Fvf1TkSI

Weffer, L. (2007, January 8). El socialismo necesita una hegemonía comunicacional. *El Nacional*, p. A/4.

Wilkinson, K. T. (2003). Language difference in the telenovela trade. *Global Media Journal, 2*(2). Retrieved from https://www.globalmediajournal.com/open-access/language-difference-in-the-telenovela-trade.php?aid=35079

Wilson, P. (2014, May 6). Venezuela's minimum wage hike is no match for inflation. *Businessweek*. Retrieved from http://www.businessweek.com/articles/2014-05-06/venezuelas-minimum-wage-hike-is-no-match-for-inflation

6 Status of institutional advertising in Venezuela during 1999–2018

Agrivalca Canelón S.

Abstract

The purpose of this analysis is to offer a retrospective examination of the behavior of the Bolivarian Government of Venezuela, qua advertiser, in the period between 1999 and 2018. This chapter looks at the evolution of institutional advertising deployed during those two decades, examining it under the prism of the so-called Government Communication Routines (RCG, for its acronym in Spanish), and the creation and development of the "Bolivarian Government Brand" through three perspectives:

1 The economic perspective, with a focus on the financial investment, assuming as a premise the government's condition as the country's main advertiser.
2 The political perspective, focused on the public character of communication, considering the importance of the administration of institutional advertising under the criteria of equity and transparency, outside the pretensions of (direct and indirect) political control and censorship.
3 The symbolic perspective, focused around government image-related campaigns, which have represented communicational milestones during the time period under consideration, whose iconographic references support management brands, creative syntheses, and visual narratives with ideological content for the mobilization of forces both domestic and international.

This analysis uses the concepts "Advertiser State," as proposed by García (2001), and "Myth of Government," advanced by Riorda (2006), and seeks to contribute to our understanding of the discourses and narratives of the nation in order to justify and legitimize the authoritarian character of political regimes (Canelón, 2008).

Introduction

Based on the theoretical contributions of Ortega (1977) and Cortés (2007), the label of institutional advertising entails those forms of communication that are produced, directed, and disseminated by entities whose ownership is public. Furthermore, these entities are focused on the creation, organization, and distribution of services for society (i.e., ministries, Central Administration agencies) as well as on the generation of values and attitudes aimed at improving citizens' relations with each other, and between them and their social, physical, and natural environment.

Institutional advertising points to a direct communication route promoted by the State at different levels (national, regional, or local) to keep the population informed about decisions, processes, and government actions pertaining to public policies. In consequence, independently of the mode of expression chosen to channel institutional advertising, it is essential that the messages are truly useful, relevant, and comprehensible, in order to provide citizens with complete and updated information, which is based on real and concrete public communication needs.

It is understood that, as the public state sector is the inherent context for the issuance of institutional advertising, this distinctive feature determines its purposes and scope based on the achievement of the "general interest" (Pineda & Rey, 2009). At this stage, any information about institutional advertising is public information. Therefore, its access constitutes a fundamental right that the authorities have the duty to protect and that exceeds the mandate to merely satisfy public demands.

Considering that institutional advertising uses the same spaces and times as commercial advertising, official entities appeal to media and formats that ensure better access and dissemination of information among the population. To do so, they consider factors that are inherent to the effectiveness of the message such as target audience profile, eligible media (press, radio, television, cinema, internet), circulation measurement (certified by collegiate institutes), and the going purchasing rates for spaces and/or times.

Additionally, the fact that the advertising of governmental institutions uses public funds for financing implies compliance with parameters of transparency and accountability. As such, the State is committed to informing the citizens concerning the pre-advertisement (terms of service, media offer, approved budgets, costs, payment methods, delivery time); the development of the campaign (goals, duration, message contents, disclosure platforms); and, finally, the income (expenses by organizations, campaigns, items, and means; advertising agencies involved; final product quality).

A statement like this inscribes institutional advertising as the most comprehensive architecture of government political communication, making it consubstantial of the democratic regimes that must explain the orientations of their plans, the results derived from the application of its measures, and the political circumstances that define decision-making, to obtain support and build social consensus (Riorda, 2006).

Riorda (2008) indicates that institutional advertising embodies a substantive part of the Government Communication Routines (RCG), which reflect the communication style of governments, configuring ways of perceiving and assimilating their image based on "communication facts" which become vehiculated through speeches or advertising spots. This requires paying attention to the conditions under which institutional advertising is issued, taking into consideration the nature of the State and the risk of transgressing the norms according to the needs of promoting the image of itself, the president and her/his team, or the government party and its candidates (Fernández, 2009).

When public interest is subject to subordination of the desire for notoriety and positioning of the dominant political group, institutional advertising distorts its purposes in a way that often borders on propaganda (Ruiz, 2009). Hence, the hybrid that Pineda and Rey (2009) call Propagandistic Institutional Advertising is used as a tool for self-promotion and electoral weapon by quite a few states in the world, something that is not foreign to Venezuela between 1999 and today.

In fact, when characterizing the RCG implemented by President Hugo Chávez throughout his mandate, some scholars have coined the analytical categories "Communicator State" (Bisbal, 2009) and "Government diffuser Propaganda" (Hernández, 2012). Based on these approaches, the analyses of the state of communication in Venezuela have addressed issues such as media ownership, the professional practice of journalism, the legal framework and its regulatory implications, freedom of expression and the right to information, the public service of radio and television, alternative media, telecommunications, and budgets in the culture sector.

A less common topic on the debate agenda, however, has been institutional advertising, surpassed by the commercial aspect within the set of disciplinary studies on advertising. Despite the importance it has as a form of communication of public administrations (Cortés, 2011), this seeming lacuna serves to undertake, in the following lines, a journey that describes the weight given to and the role played by institutional advertising as part of government communication strategies applied by Hugo Chávez and, later, by Nicolás Maduro.

"Advertiser State": advertising, investment, and power

The analysis of the persuasion component within the RCG of the Bolivarian government requires a comprehensive reading, especially considering the exponential increase verified during the last decade in the institutional advertising quotas. Not surprisingly, the assertion that the Venezuelan State has become one of the most important advertisers in the country, to not say the main one, when quantifying the value of the air minutes of its televisual, filmic, and radio broadcasts; besides the space occupied in newspapers, magazines, and billboards.

Without a doubt, following the events of April 2002, media acquired a strategic character for the Venezuelan government in relation to both ideological confrontation and cultural modeling. This new vision, officially proclaimed on January 8, 2007 by the director of Telesur at that time, Andrés Izarra, received the denomination of the "communication and informational hegemony of the State" (Weffer, 2007). The approach supported efforts aimed at the management of public media, the creation of a national system of communitarian and alternative media, and the promotion of independent audiovisual production. Special mention should be made of the aspiration to strengthen the State media network with new technology, infrastructure, and personnel, in addition to acquiring new ones, favoring a policy of progressive breakdown of the concentration of media managed by the private sector (Pezzella, 2009).

Communicational hegemony involved not only the accumulation of information and entertainment media, but also the search for omnipresence (Morales, 2014). The analysis of Ministry of Communication and Information (MINCI) budgets from 2010 to today shows that approximately 65% of the organization's resources devoted to advertising-propaganda are distributed in advertising guidelines; preparation of books, brochures, posters, flyers, and leaflets; design and development of advertising campaigns, press notices, and writing scripts for radio and television (Bisbal, 2016).

According to the data provided by the Media Certification Committee of the National Association of Advertisers (ANDA), the Venezuelan Federation of Advertising Agencies (FEVAP), and the Venezuelan Advertising Institute of Caracas (IVP), the Bolivarian government's advertising behavior reveals an absolute dominance of television advertising since 2007 (Moreno, 2012 as cited in Canelón,

2016). Precisely, at that time, Hugo Chávez promoted the 21st century socialism as a pillar of his government program for the period 2007–13 (Observatorio Socialista de Venezuela-Instituto de Altos Estudios Diplomáticos Pedro Gual, 2007).

Given this particular aspect, it is convenient to highlight the existence of three tools inserted in the RCG introduced by President Hugo Chávez, which imply the advertising capitalization of resources, privileges, and public attributions in electoral campaigns: national radio and television mandatory transmissions ("chains"), programs like "Aló Presidente," and free broadcasts (Alerta Electoral, 2012). In this sense, spending grew, especially, during the prelude and the development of electoral processes (national, regional, or local), distorting institutional advertising with propaganda. Additionally, with the aspiration to achieve a uniform presence across the country, the government opted for regional and alternative media (television stations, radio stations, and newspapers) (Ventana Bolivariana, 2006).

In the meantime, government entities also experimented with new advertising formats, such as self-adhering gigantographies for Petróleos de Venezuela, S.A. (PDVSA), some ministries, and National Integrated Service for the Administration of Customs Duties and Taxes (SENIAT) (Guaglianone, 2008). The National Telephone Company of Venezuela (CANTV) did the same with announcements at bus stops, posters, and digital displays in public transport units (Rodríguez, 2007).

In 2009, the number of companies under the tutelage of the State increased. As a result, according to AGB reports, the National Government ranked among the top five television advertisers behind companies like Empresas Polar, Procter & Gamble, Cervecería Regional, and Colgate Palmolive. This trajectory continued in 2010, according to the ANDA-Fevap Media Certification Committee report, in which the Bolivarian government stands out as the largest television advertiser (seconded by Procter & Gamble and Polar), also leading radio investment (flanked by Polar, Procter & Gamble, and Movistar) (Adlatina, 2011).

The aforementioned source notes that, around 2011, advertising spending of public entities tended to concentrate, in addition to television, in print press (together with banking, services, CPG, beverages, and automotive), radio (with categories such as telecommunications, supermarkets, and fast food), and outdoor advertising (standard posters, double fences, and gigantographies) (Domínguez, 2012).

With the arrival of 2012, the growth of official advertising in all the media was notorious. The National Government invested Bs. 530 million in television, circulating pieces alluding to the achievements of social missions (especially the Great Housing Mission Venezuela). Meanwhile, among the top 20 advertisers in the press, seven were public entities (headed by the MINCI, PDVSA, and the Bicentennial Bank), apart from the ruling party (United Socialist Party of Venezuela, – PSUV). Regarding billboards, the amount of investment by government entities reached Bs. 787 million (standard and compact formats of road advertising with electoral contents), even exceeding the amount reserved to radio (Bs. 760 million). Likewise, the Bolivarian government bought spaces in cinema for the transmission of institutional videos in favor of the Revolution.

In short, in the words of Javier Salas, General Manager of the ANDA-Fevap Media Certification Committee:

> [...] The retraction in advertising investment that characterized the private sector generated available spaces that were used by the advanced of propaganda of the Government, to which, by October of last year, CNE campaigns were added, official bodies such as governorates and mayors, political parties and candidates [...].
> (Entorno Inteligente, 2013)

The trend continued once President Nicolás Maduro assumed the presidency in 2013, with the MINCI having a budget of 9.5 billion Bolívares, in addition to the 11 billion Bolívares obtained via additional Parliamentary-approved appropriations. In 2015, the MINCI budget increased 118.7% compared to that of 2014 (from 1.1 billion Bolívares to 2.4 billion). Nearly 73.7% of that amount corresponded to exclusive use in official propaganda, as it was an election year. For the development of information campaigns, MINCI had 432 million Bolívares, distributed as follows: campaigns (Bs. 178 million), coverage and dissemination of presidential management (Bs. 81 million), dissemination of social interest's content through printed and digital platforms (Bs. 90 million), and optimization of the transmission of events of national interest (Bs. 81 million) (Vásquez, 2016).

The increase in resources for propaganda in 2015 was in response to the creation of the Venezuelan Advertising Agency (AVP), overseen by the MINCI, with the mission of planning, producing, and disseminating the State's advertising campaigns. During that year, the AVP released 4,464,600 advertising pieces through different media (print, television, digital, and billboards), an unprecedented record for the National Public Administration (Bisbal, 2016).

Considering this evidence, in addition to the "Communicating State" and the "Government diffuser Propaganda," in the case of

Venezuela, it is possible to recognize a third facet: the "Advertiser State." This role gives it a determining potential to the advertising investment done by public entities, causing a direct impact on the performance of the media, in the case of the exercise of their inherent functions to comptroller management, freedom of expression, and the right to information. From this point of view, for the government, the activity of informing about public policies, the results of the public administration, and, in general, about the "achievements" of government management acquires a persuasive and strategic character.

Advertising and collective imaginaries

The analysis of the RCG as applied by the administration of Hugo Chávez implies taking into consideration the influence of cultural matrices and symbolic components on the political-ideological process, which has resulted in the production of meanings and values with a wide impact on the handling of collective actions. Not in vain, according to Acosta (2013), symbolic intermediation is the simplest way to convey a discourse, bring together common meanings, evoke strong emotions, and synthesize a complex political and social reality, favoring ideological identification and relationship of leaders with the most politically active groups.

In the words of Romero (2006), since 1999, the Hugo Chávez administration installed a new politeia based on the offer of a national project that broke with the democratic past established in 1958 (the Fourth Republic), in order to build the new "political model" of the "Bolivarian people's democracy" (the Fifth Republic) (Biardeau, 2009). To do so, it appealed to the symbolic references of the military and patriotic force (Hernández, 2007) to direct the people toward the objectives of the Revolution (Palacio, 2008) and the unfortuitous approval of the modification of the national symbols through the reform of the National Flag, Shield and Anthem Law, published in Official Gazette No. 38,394 of March 9, 2006. However, the most important transformation was the change in the name of the country from "Republic of Venezuela" to "Bolivarian Republic of Venezuela."

Based on these milestones, Acosta (2013) distinguishes two stages in Bolivarian government iconography. The first is marked by the genesis of the revolutionary process in 1999 and linked to a collective construction in which a spontaneous heterogeneity of images prevailed. The second, crystallized after the 2006 presidential elections and extended until today, tends to institutionalize symbolic elements.

Following this orientation, the graphic criteria of the government's image were standardized (Pérez, 2010).

In 2005, an institutional logo had already appeared with the colors of the national flag and the slogan *"Venezuela ahora es de todos"* ("Venezuela now belongs to everyone"). In 2008, a communication campaign was launched that included the expression *"del Poder Popular"* ("of Popular Power"), with the purpose of projecting proximity to the most vulnerable social groups. At the same time, the formalization of the visual identity of the State materialized through the manual of "Graphic Image of the Bolivarian Government of Venezuela of Basic Applications" (2006). In this sense, the ultimate intention was aimed at uniting in a single graphic representation the work of all official ministries and agencies, inspiring a single government speech.

The distinctive sign selected for print advertising (print ads, banners, posters, and flyers), outdoor (billboards), and audiovisual (end caps of television spots) was the patriotic tricolor waving from left to right, accompanied with the phrase *"Gobierno Bolivariano de Venezuela"* ("Bolivarian Government of Venezuela") and the name of associated Ministry, both always located in the lower left corner. Likewise, the logo theme was included with the institutional slogan *"Con Chávez el Pueblo es el Gobierno"* ("With Chávez the People are the Government").

In 2010, a new graphic proposal emerged in the context of the bicentennial celebration of the Venezuelan independence, which motivated the design of the commemorative logo "200 Bicentennial" ("200 Bicentenario"), in order to represent the 200 years of the independence movement and pay tribute to Simón Bolívar. For this reason, the use of the equestrian figure as "an example of struggle and resistance" fused the fatherland with "our American" (Ministerio del Poder Popular para la Comunicación y la Información, 2010: 28).

In 2012, the "Venezuelan Heart" ("Corazón Venezolano") campaign replaced the "200 Bicentennial" image. The new communication initiative was leveraged "in the close relationship [...] between the management led by President Hugo Chávez and the Venezuelan people," with a focus on "transformative work to consolidate the purposes established in the Simón Bolívar National Project." In this vein, the identifier proposed to suggest the shape of the heart consisted of a tape whose "tricolor route gives a sense of progression, of upward and forward direction," honoring three conceptual elements: optimism, inclusion, and permanent work (Ministerio del Poder Popular para la Comunicación y la Información, 2012: 11).

The government communication campaign "Venezuelan Heart" came to close the *continuum* of signs and slogans that, from 2005 to

2013, with the Bolivarian Government of Venezuela logo, condensed the messages (promises and goals) disseminated by the Executive Power in the person of Hugo Chávez, operating as an identity support (visual and aural) of the institutions of the Venezuelan State. This provided constant visibility in traditional and non-traditional media, positioning the work of the Revolution with "creative acuity and political intentions" (Ministerio del Poder Popular para la Comunicación y la Información, 2012: 9–11), although using, according to Pérez (2010), hyper-production of pieces articulated with a populist and authoritarian discourse, not at all free of propaganda.

After the passing of Hugo Chávez, the official government image campaign for the period 2012–13, which premiered on May 14, 2013 by Nicolás Maduro as President of the Bolivarian Republic of Venezuela, maintained the previous tone, inspired in the commemoration of the "Admirable Campaign" ("La Campaña Admirable") bicentennial (Moreno, 2013). The same happened with the identity proposal "Bicentennial Youth" ("Juventud Bicentenaria") (Ministerio del Poder Popular para la Comunicación y la Información, 2014: 2). The recurrence to meanings built on the nationalist epic returned in 2016 with the campaign in honor of the birth of General Ezequiel Zamora, accompanied by the slogans "Victorious Rebellion" ("Rebelión Victoriosa") and "United Patriots know how to win" ("Patriotas unidos sabemos vencer").

These communication initiatives of the Bolivarian government have coexisted in parallel with the myth around the figure of Hugo Chávez, reinforced as a personal brand in order to build trust among the followers and support the government management of Nicolás Maduro (Morao, 2014).

From an advertising perspective, the construction of a "brand narrative" (brand statement) of the national project, whose axes are the revolutionary, the national, the civic-military, and the popular, is linked to a conception of the "Bolivarian democracy" (Biardeau, 2009). Hence, the development of a brand architecture gives direction to an imaginary that defines the existing ("what is" and "what is not"), the desirable ("where society should go"), and what is possible ("how far society can go") (Molina, 2002).

Thus, Hugo Chávez gave new meanings to common discursive categories, generating sub-brands of the main story (Esté, 2006: 52, quoted in Bisbal, 2009), through the slogans "Chávez is like you" ("*Chávez es como tú*") and "With Chávez, the people are the Government" ("*Con Chávez manda el pueblo*") (Bisbal, 2010). Consequently, propaganda and censorship protected under the umbrella of institutional advertising establish a "political make" from the symbolic world, communicating it through a "myth of government" that supports the general project and the guidelines of the management policies (Riorda, 2008), and facilitates the movement toward utopian discourse (Narvaja, 2008).

Perhaps, the best advertising pieces that reflect the "myth of government" of President Hugo Chávez are the television spots broadcast in 2011 and 2012 (coinciding with the latter year's presidential campaign), which show the achievements of the Bolivarian government. The first one, entitled "Venezuela Satellite," emphasized the country's food and technological sovereignty; hence, the special allusion to the "Venezuela Products" (*"Productos Venezuela"*), the "Great Mission AgroVenezuela" (*"Gran Misión AgroVenezuela"*), and "Los Andes Dairy" (*"Lácteos Los Andes"*) added to the initiatives "Venirauto," "Canaimita," "Vergatario 2," the "Orinoquia Bridge," and the "Great Housing Mission Venezuela" (*"Gran Misión Vivienda Venezuela"*). The second video, entitled "Venezuela, achievements since Simón Bolívar Satellite to the Children's Cardiology," starts with a shot from outer space that quickly lowers to Earth to show each of the public services provided by the Venezuelan government to citizens in their daily lives. Specifically, the images show the "Direct Television to the Home" (*"Televisión Directa al Hogar"*), "My Well-Equipped House" (*"Mi Casa Bien Equipada"*), the "Great Mission to Know and Work" (*"Gran Misión Saber y Trabajo"*), the "Bicentennial Supply Network" (*"Red de Abastos Bicentenario"*), and the "State Railway Institute" (*"Instituto Ferroviario del Estado"*), among others. The sequence closes with the cover of the official image "Venezuelan Heart." Both pieces share as background music the popular song "Alma Llanera," authored by Pedro Elías Gutiérrez, arranged for the Simón Bolívar Youth Orchestra, under the direction of Gustavo Dudamel (Morao, 2012).

Without a doubt, these representations within the framework of the social imaginary legitimize the action of the "enunciator-government" and magnify its figure, appearing, at least in a first reading, that the Bolivarian government is a good manager of public resources and assumes the obligation of service to its citizens. This highlights their competence to act and achieve a better society ("The Supreme Social Happiness" – *"La Suprema Felicidad Social"*), translated into a "power to do" and a "know-how": public works, education, health, housing, transportation, agricultural production and manufacturing, food distribution and technology.

In short, subject to this evidence, the "utopian discourse" should not be understood simply as an advertising communication strategy or its content; rather, it constitutes the latent structures that give meaning and establish the legitimacy frameworks of the different public policies that were implemented, identifying management and defining the semiotic field of government communication (Cejudo, 2008). To all these, the myth of the government influences the decoding process and, therefore, helps people interpret reality according to the interests promoted by the government through its communication (Cabás & Delle Donne, 2010). In this context, "brand management" embodies empirical evidence of the "myth of government," crystallized in a creative synthesis and advertising brief.

Bibliographic References

Acosta, Y. (2013). Elementos simbólicos de la confrontación política venezolana. In M. Bisbal (Ed.), *La Política y sus tramas. Miradas desde la Venezuela del presente* (pp. 26–49). UCAB-Konrad Adenauer Stiftung.

Adlatina. (2011, August 30). La inversión publicitaria en Venezuela se mantuvo en comparación con 2010. http://www.adlatina.com/negocios/la-inversi%C3%B3n-publicitaria-en-venezuela-se-mantuvo-en-comparaci%C3B3n-con-2010

Alerta Electoral. (2012). Un candidato compite contra el Estado. http://alertaelectoral.blogspot.com/2012/07/un-candidato-compite-contra-el-estado.html

Biardeau, J. (2009). Del árbol de las tres raíces al 'Socialismo Bolivariano del Siglo XXI' ¿Una nueva narrativa ideológica de emancipación? *Revista Venezolana de Economía y Ciencias Sociales*, 15(1), 57–113.

Bisbal, M. (2009). La comunicación masiva como política del gobierno de Hugo Chávez Frías. In M. Bisbal (Ed.), *Hegemonía y control comunicacional* (pp. 23–60). Editorial Alfa.

Bisbal, M. (2010). Vivimos hoy una situación límite: medios, cultura y nación. *Comunica. Revista Latinoamericana de Comunicación Social*, 1(1), 133–49.

Bisbal, M. (2016). La hegemonía comunicacional desde el nuevo gobierno, el de Nicolás Maduro. In M. Bisbal (Ed.), *La comunicación bajo asedio. Balance de 17 años* (pp. 377–415). AB UCAB Ediciones.

Cabás, P., & Delle Donne, F. (2010, May 5–6). *La construcción del mito de gobierno desde las políticas de Inclusión Social* [ponencia]. IV Congreso Latinoamericano de Opinión Pública de WAPOR, Belo Horizonte, Brasil.

Canelón, A. (2008). Estado socialista con Marca Bolivariana. *Comunicación. Estudios venezolanos de comunicación*. First quarter, (141), 27–35.

Canelón, A. (2016). El estado anunciante 14 años del "mito de gobierno" de Hugo Chávez. In M. Bisbal (Ed.), *La comunicación bajo asedio. Balance de 17 años* (pp. 94–130). AB UCAB Ediciones.

Cejudo, G. (2008). *Discurso y políticas públicas: enfoque constructivista* (Documento de Trabajo N° 205). Centro de Investigación y Docencia Económicas (CIDE). http://libreriacide.com/librospdf/DTAP-205.pdf

Cortés, A. (2007). *Cultura de Paz y Publicidad Institucional*. Alcalá Grupo Editorial.
Cortés, A. (2011). La Publicidad Institucional en España. Una década en Perspectiva. *Revista Razón y Palabra*, (75), 1–23.
Domínguez, C. (2012, June 11). Inversión Publicitaria: crecimiento fue inferior a la inflación. *Gerente.com*. https://web.archive.org/web/20121017201723/ Entorno Inteligente. (2013, May 6). Propaganda oficial gana espacios de la publicidad del sector privado. http://www.entornointeligente.com/articulo2/1447639/Propaganda-oficial-gana-espacios-de-la-publicidad-del-sector-privado
Fernández, A. (2009). Tendencias de las acciones de RRPP desarrolladas en instituciones públicas de carácter político. *Revista Latina de Comunicación Social*, 12 (64), 248–61.
García, M. (2001). *Publicidad Institucional: el Estado Anunciante*. Universidad de Málaga.
Guaglianone, J. (2008, March 18). El Metro y la publicidad neocapitalista. *Alterinfos*. http://www.alterinfos.org/spip.php?article2124
Hernández, A. (2007). La identidad visual de la revolución. *El Universal*, Cuerpo 3, p. 13.
Hernández, G. (2012, March 10). Comentarios a la ponencia "El Estado-Comunicador y sus comunicaciones: ¿comunicaciones de Servicio Público?". Encuentro de Organizaciones Sociales (EOS), Caracas, Venezuela.
Ministerio del Poder Popular para la Comunicación y la Información. (2010). *Manual de Uso Logo Gobierno Bolivariano de Venezuela – 200 años*. http://www.minci.gob.ve/
Ministerio del Poder Popular para la Comunicación y la Información. (2012). *Manual de Imagen de Gobierno. Período 2012–2013*. http://www.minci.gob.ve/
Ministerio del Poder Popular para la Comunicación y la Información. (2014). *Logo para los 200 años de la Batalla de La Victoria. Juventud Bicentenaria*. http://www.minci.gob.ve/
Molina, J. (2002). *Imágenes colectivas y propuestas ideológicas del Estado y lo Público en Colombia a finales del siglo XX. Estudio de caso de la Reforma Constitucional de 1991. Elemento para pensar una nueva reforma política*. Escuela Superior de Administración Pública (ESAP).
Morales, M. (2014, November 17). Con m de millardo se escribe hegemonía comunicacional. *Monitoreo Ciudadano*. http://monitoreociudadano.org/yomonitoreo/2014/11/con-m-de-millardo-se-escribe-hegemonia-comunicacional/
Morao, J. (2012, July 10). Publicidad gubernamental bolivariana resumida en un spot televisivo. *Jingleelectoral.com*. http://jingleelectoral.com/tag/propaganda-gubernamental/
Morao, J. (2014, April 21). La épica de la propaganda. *Jingleelectoral.com*. https://web.archive.org/web/20140722205027/
Moreno, F. (2013, May 14). Presentado logo oficial para conmemorar bicentenario de la Campaña Admirable. *Correo del Orinoco*. http://www.

correodelorinoco.gob.ve/presentado-logo-oficial-para-conmemorar-bicentenario-campana-admirable/
Moreno, S. (2012, May 26). Cierre de RCTV no mermó la publicidad, pero sí la audiencia. *Elmundo.com.*
Narvaja, E. (2008). *El discurso latinoamericanista de Hugo Chávez.* Editorial Biblos.
Observatorio Socialista de Venezuela - Instituto de Altos Estudios Diplomáticos Pedro Gual. (2007). *Moral y Luces: el Tercer Gran Motor Constituyente.* http://institutopedrogual.mppre.gob.ve/
Ortega, E. (1997). *La Comunicación Publicitaria.* Editorial Pirámide.
Palacio, J. (2008). Manejo de la simbología en el ascenso y consolidación de Hugo Chávez en el poder [tesis de grado, Universidad Colegio Mayor de Nuestra Señora del Rosario]. Repositorio Institucional. https://repository.urosario.edu.co/handle/10336/1105
Pérez, E. (2010, January 26). Una mirada al diseño gráfico del Gobierno Bolivariano.*Analitica.com.*http://www.analitica.com/va/arte/dossier/7787966.asp
Pezzella, S. (2009). Gobierno bolivariano, marca registrada. *Veneconomía*, 26(12), 1–5.
Pineda, A., & Rey, J. (2009). Propaganda y Publicidad Institucional: algunas consideraciones teóricas. *Questiones Publicitarias: Monografía 3 "Publicidad Institucional,"* 2° etapa, 9–32. doi:10.5565/rev/qp.113
Riorda, M. (2006). Hacia un modelo de comunicación gubernamental para el consenso. In D. Fernández, L. Elizalde & M. Riorda (Eds.), *La construcción del consenso. Gestión de la comunicación gubernamental* (pp. 17–142). La Crujía Ediciones.
Riorda, M. (2008). "Gobierno bien, pero comunico mal": análisis de las Rutinas de la Comunicación Gubernamental. *Revista del CLAD Reforma y Democracia,* (40), 1–15.
Rodríguez, D. (2007). Telecomunicaciones: la nueva red socialista. *Dinero XIX Aniversario,* (226), 77–79.
Romero, C. (2006). *Jugando con el globo. La política exterior de Hugo Chávez.* Ediciones B.
Ruiz, F. (2009). El Estado es el Producto. Publicidad Institucional, rutinas discursivas e ideología de Estado. *Questiones Publicitarias: Monografía 3 "Publicidad Institucional,"* 2° etapa, 268–93. doi:10.5565/rev/qp.113
Vásquez, A. (2016). Con Maduro el presupuesto del MINCI creció 519% para promocionar al gobierno. In M. Bisbal (Ed.), *La comunicación bajo asedio. Balance de 17 años* (pp. 447–51). AB UCAB Ediciones.
Ventana Bolivariana. (2006, March 29). Ministro Lara afina estrategia comunicacionalconorganismosdelEstado.http://www.ventanabolivariana.org.ve/index.php/Ministro-Lara-afina-estrategia-comunicacional-con-organismos-del-Estado.html
Weffer, L. (2007, January 8). El socialismo necesita una hegemonía comunicacional. *El Nacional,* Cuerpo A, p. 4.

7 The return of the Caudillos in the digital age – changing hegemony and *Media Caesarism*

Continuities and changes in the news media landscape under the *Chavismo*

Jairo Lugo-Ocando and Andrés Cañizález

Abstract
Over the past two decades, the *Chavista* regime has been able to survive all attempts to outset it from power. From military uprisings, public mass protests, and even the possibility of US intervention all have but failed in trying to undermine the grip to power that the current regime holds. There is little doubt that the use of coercion has been central in this exercise of power. Something that has included the systematic assassination, jailing, and forcible disappearance of dissidents. Nevertheless, it is not less true that the *Chavismo* also kept a substantial number of followers who have remained loyal to what they call the *Bolivarian Revolution*. So, despite losing the 2015 parliamentarian election in an overwhelming defeat that was seen as an extensive erosion of its political base, the regime – now under Nicolas Maduro – clings to power despite US sanctions, scarcity of basic goods, struggle to juggle with a dollarized economy and in the face of fuel shortages and power cuts. The question is, therefore, what keeps the political base of the Chavismo mobilized and a great segment of the opposition paralyzed? The answer, as we suggest in this chapter, is that the regime has been successfully able to build a new media and cultural hegemony that changed the terms of reference for many people in that country and that helps its subdue attempts to outset it from power.

Introduction

Over the decades running from 1998 and until the late Hugo Rafael Chávez Frías (1954–2013) was elected President of Venezuela, a series of experts, scholars, and members of the public had complained about the firm grip that a small group of privately owned media outlets had upon the country in terms of dominating the news agenda and shaping public opinion (Aguirre & Bisbal, 1981; Bisbal, 1994; Cañizález, 1991; Mujica, 2008 [1982]). Many of these scholars called this a market-driven media hegemony that provided the power basis for the two main political parties – namely *Acción Democrática* (AD) and *Comité de Organización Política Electoral Independiente* (COPEI) – and help perpetuated a system of privileges set by the economic elites represented in their guild the *Federación de Cámaras y Asociaciones de Comercio y Producción de Venezuela* (*Fedecámaras*). Indeed, this arrangement that operated since 1958 under the denomination of *Pacto de Punto Fijo* was a formal arrangement arrived in the main political parties not only to accept the results of the first presidential elections in order to preserve the new democratic regime and also an alliance with other actors such as the Catholic Church and *Fedecámaras* in order to provide political stability to the new regime (López-Maya, Calcaño, & Maingón, 1989; Naím & Piñango, 1986).

To be sure, the period between 1958 and 1998 was characterized by the dominance of these main political parties, which exercise political power but mainly through hegemony (Lugo-Ocando & Romero, 2003; Ramos-Jiménez, 1999), although they also had to use coercion to confront internal and external enemies such as guerilla and terrorist groups (Lugo-Ocando, 2007; Wickham-Crowley, 1992). Hegemony, nevertheless, was central in sustaining liberal democracy in that country despite very important gaps in terms of access and participation in power by a variety of sectors and actors.

By hegemony in this chapter we refer to Gramsci's conceptualization as how elites can command cultural, moral, and ideological power with the support of subaltern groups. We do subscribe to the view that in these circumstances it is based on the function that the leading group is the nucleus of economic activity. This by "convincing" the subaltern groups not only to follow but also to actively enhance the power of the elites, the latter are able to reach an equilibrium between consent and coercion in ways that they can remain in control without substantial resistance or struggle. The dominant class can then rule with the consent of subordinate masses. This hegemony supposes the leading role of the dominant class in the economy, which were able, through culture, to set forth a dominant ideology and consciousness (Gramsci, 2005 [1935]; Mouffe, 2014).

In the case of the pre-Chávez era, this hegemony took the form of a centralized, client-based (*clientelar*) national-state, which used the oil revenue to subdue social demands by providing indirect subsidies in a mass scale and developing an extensive network of political patronage and corruption (Gates, 2010; Parker, 2005). The system in place permitted the two main political parties to alternate power while catering for a private sector that was heavily dependent on subsidies and protectionism, and workers unions that were overall co-opted by the political parties and used as tools to advance their own power agenda. All of these were achieved, thanks to increasing oil revenues, which allowed the elites to create an "illusion of social harmony" (Naím & Piñango, 1986).

The main media outlets were part of this hegemonic scheme and help the elites to exercise power through cultural hegemonism and dominance of the media sphere. Newspapers, radio networks, and television networks were closely aligned with protecting the overall economic and political arrangement, although with important tensions among them (Lugo-Ocando, 2008; Lugo-Ocando & Romero, 2003). To be sure, the communicational hegemony exercised by the privately owned and commercially driven mainstream media in Venezuela became particularly acute once Chávez came to power as tensions between the new regime and exiting elites were exacerbated (Lugo-Ocando & Romero, 2003). In the coup d'état of April 11, 2002 that briefly ousted Chávez from power the media played a fundamental role not only in siding in favor of the de facto regime lead by Pedro Carmona, but in trying (unsuccessfully) to make sure that people did not mobilize in favor of Chávez. As Andrés Cañizález has pointed out, the news media will have one day to give account for the very dubious and unethical role it played in those days, particularly because of the silence they kept in a crucial moment when impartial reporting of news was more needed (Cañizález, 2002, 2016).

Over the past two decades, the *Chavista* regime survived all attempts to outset it from power – from military uprisings, public mass protests, and even the possibility of US intervention. One way or another, both Chávez and his successor Nicolás Maduro managed to fight attacks from all quarters even in the face of growing unpopularity and mass unrest. The use of coercion has been central in this exercise of power and the systematic assassination, jailing, and forcible disappearance of dissidents has been widely documented by the United Nations' High Commissioner, Michelle Bachelet, who in her report compiled substantial evidence of these violations.

Equally true is that the regime expanded the traditional client-based function of the state to levels never seen before with a series of social programs that range from food distribution to assistance to the needy in the poorest areas as well as scholarships for adult education and the construction of housing across the countries, among others. Numbers on these programs have been disputed both by local experts and by international agencies and it is very doubtful that many of the claims made by the government in relation to their reach can be somehow substantiated by evidence other than self-produced statistics by the same government (Jankovic, Colin, Ari, & Haidacher, 2019; Penfold-Becerra, 2007; Rodríguez, Morales, & Monaldi-Marturet, 2012). Nevertheless, these social programs remain pivotal to keep in line key constituencies as well as to reinforce a still powerful metaphor for propaganda and power, both at home and abroad (Carosio, 2016; Maingon, 2016; Sotomayor, 2019).

However, it is not less true that the *Chavismo* also keeps a substantial number of followers who remain loyal to what they call the *Bolivarian Revolution*. So, despite losing the 2015 election in an overwhelming defeat that was seen as an extensive erosion of its political base, the regime clings to power with still important support in some key constituencies that day after day see their income shrink, face long lines to buy basic goods, struggle to juggle with a dollarized economy, and are subject to power cuts and scarcity of medicine, water, and even petrol in the country that holds the richest oil reserves in the planet. The question is, therefore, what keeps the political base mobilized? The answer is that the regime was successfully able to build a new media and cultural hegemony that changed the terms of reference for many people in that country.

Construction of a new hegemony

One of the central communication tasks developed during the time of the *Chavismo* in power has been about establishing a new communicational hegemony, which subordinates the traditional liberal democratic ethos of commercial plurality to the need of incorporating alternative voices and news agendas that are supportive of the regime in power (Cañizález, 2014) as this is seen as a way of bringing the *popular* – as in grassroots – into the public realm. This included reformulating the legal framework in which the commercial and privately owned media had traditionally operated by discretionally withdrawing broadcasting license while re-awarding them to political acolytes or government-run networks, and using the security forces and the judicial system to threaten, imprison, and exile journalists and private media owners into leaving their jobs and/or the country, selling their media outlets to allies of the regime, and overall implementing measures that unequivocally led to self-censorship and bowing to the political power in a scale never seen before (Atwood, 2006; Corrales, 2015; Knight & Tribin, 2019).

The change in the composition and nature of the media ecology that had been formed since 1958 and that had until then help underpinned power for the former elites of the previous regime –referred to as Fourth Republic – was disguised under the formulation of new legal framework and the reorientation of policies and resources allocated toward communication. All this was done under the façade of "democratizing" the media sphere, something that for years activists, experts, and scholars had been crying out loud for (Aguirre & Bisbal, 1981; Bisbal, 1994; Cañizález, 1991; Pasquali, 1980). The end result, however, was instead a blunt justification to displace or subdue the old media actors into the regime's sphere of influence and control.

The new hegemony was already established in the years before the arrival of Nicolás Maduro, Chávez successor, into power and certainly since then it has muted into a far less subtle form of authoritarian and coercive control. However, for decades preceding, the government of the late Hugo Chávez gradually established his grip upon communication and a culture in no uncertain terms and used coercion in numerous occasions, which goes to the grain of some trying to draw a line between the administration of Chávez and Maduro. In the past two decades, the *Chavista* regime has developed a media and cultural apparatus that broke the relationship with the old elites – making media owners to sell their shares from media outlets or just closing them down – and transformed communications and community relations in ways that they became subordinated to the *Bolivarian Revolution* project.

This new hegemonic setting, implemented by the *Chavismo*, was called by Venezuelan journalist and social commentator, Boris Muñoz, as "Media Caesarism" (Sánchez, 2016) in a clear allusion to the theory of "Democratic Caesarism." The latter term was first used by Laureano Vallenilla Lanz (1991 [1919]), one of the top ministers and political advisors for the dictator Juan Vicente Gómez (1857–1935). It makes historical reference to the government of Julio César in Rome, which was an absolutist regime but it came to power to allegedly save the nation. Perhaps the best characterization of the concept is that of the Italian Marxist thinker Antonio Gramsci (2005 [1935]), who pointed out that Caesarism always expresses the arbitrary solution, entrusted to a great personality, of a historical and political situation characterized by a balance of forces from catastrophic perspectives. For Vallenilla Lanz (1991 [1919]), Juan Vicente Gómez, who came to power after years of civil wars, political unrest, and economic turmoil, represented exactly that; the return of order based on the conditions on the ground rather than the ideal democratic aspirations of legislator in the hope that new generations would be better prepared to undertake power in a responsible and effective manner.

The extrapolation of this notion as a way of providing a theoretical explanatory framework for the transformation of the media ecology in Venezuela is, we believe, useful in the way of understanding the new hegemonic setting. This signifies both the way the *Chavista* regime justifies its role in society in relation to re-configuring of the media landscape and what has actually happened with these same transformations in terms of polarization, plurality, and freedom of expression. Hence, one of the key aspects in this chapter is to try to develop further the conceptualization of this term.

Needless to say, the most distinctive and simple aim of the new *Chavista* media hegemony has been to consolidate power into its own hands. So, let us put aside the initial claims made by those supporting the so-called Bolivarian Revolution – or Socialism of the 21st Century – that reforms in the media system and across the spectrum were carried out to make it more democratic, accessible, and participative. With this, we are not suggesting that all efforts made were cynical attempts to take control or that the intention to democratize the media was not there at all. On the contrary, many of the key figureheads supporting the *Chavismo* were very honestly enthusiastic about the prospect of a new, more open, and overall increasingly "popular" new media ecology. One that incorporated dozens of community radio stations into the airwaves, financially and technically, supported grassroots-based television station and incentivized literally hundreds of blogs, websites, and small media outlets to give voice to the communities (Cañizalez, 2007; Porto, 2019).

However, these legislative changes were also part of broader efforts to impose power and silence its opponents. Let us not forget that these efforts also included the displacement of traditional actors, the persecution and jailing of journalists, judges, and political opponents at large as well as rescinding the broadcasting license and effectively shutting down the main television network RCTV in 2007 while threatening with jail the owner of another key opposition network, *Globovision*, as to make him sell all his shares to a government acolyte in 2013 (Cañizález & Matos-Smith, 2015).

Indeed, for the late Hugo Chávez himself, it was very important to succeed in imposing a new communicational hegemony that could help underpin the political hegemony. This to the point that some scholars have called his period as one of "Mediatized Presidency" (Cañizález, 2016). This in practice meant not only radically changing the state-run communicational apparatus, expanding the radius of power and influence over the commercial and privately owned media, but also creating direct communication channels with the public. Yes, way before the populist US President Donald J. Trump started to use Twitter to correspond directly with his constituencies, Chávez had mastered the art of broadcasting weekly and even daily in some occasions for hours while obliging all television and radio networks in the country to also broadcast live the same audiovisual feed of his program *"Aló Presidente"* (Erlich, 2005; Frajman, 2014).

Achieving *Media Caesarism*

Hence, *Media Caesarism*– or *Mediatized Caesarism* as we might also call it – is a category that not only defines the imposition of a particular form of centralized control of the media, as many dictatorships and authoritarian regimes have done in the past, but also designates a form of control over the media spectrum, which is centered around the figure of its leader and which claims that it "gives democratic voice to the people" while constructing a "popular" and Enlightened public sphere, which in ways is similar to the Nazi or Fascist models that also embraced the principle of the leader as the voice of the masses. However, contrary to Nazis and Fascism, the *Chavismo* showed a true appetite to open the airwaves and media spaces to grassroots supporters in ways that resemble the initial stage of the Soviet Revolution – referred to as the "Soviet Enlightenment," when for a brief period of time Lenin opened up the press to the masses (Chehonadskih, 2017; Lenoe, 2004).

In this sense, the regime presented itself on the media as open and accessible by not only allowing calls from the public but also making policy while on air. Indeed, the then head of state, Hugo Chávez, often issued on live television new government guidelines, announced decisions, and even changed state strategies that seemed to take even his closest collaborators by surprise. This, from our perspective, represents an official trend, which in particular falls on the figure of the president: many decisions that impact public policy do not necessarily respond to previously designed plans and programs but instead was part of the logic of a television staging, in which the space conductor, President Hugo Chávez, had enormous power to vary the script, make announcements, and make decisions without having previously agreed on the government team. Some scholars in Europe have called this the *Mediatization* of politics (Hepp, 2013; Strömbäck, 2008), which refers to how the logics of the media are superimposed upon the way we do politics and how leaders adapt policy-making and actions to the dynamics of the media.

In the case of Venezuela, we had the additional issue of "personalism," which became central under Hugo Chávez in relation to his ever presence on the small screen. However, this was not the type of "cult to personality" that scholars and observers alike underpin to the historical accounts of communist and fascist leaders such as Joseph Stalin, Benito Mussolini, Adolf Hitler, or more recently Kim Jong-un (Lim, 2015; Tucker, 1979), but instead it was more an expression of what in Latin America we have called "caudillismo."

One of the key reasons as to why we refer to the term "*Media Caesarism*" is precisely the particular setting of the *Chavismo* in relation to the notion of the *caudillo*. From the start the new hegemonic setting was highly dependent upon the strong figure of the war overlord, who as a feudal knight took care of the peasant and takes all the decisions. Indeed, the "caudillismo" has been a very important explanatory framework in Latin America and specifically in Venezuela since its independence from Spain (Irwin & Micett, 2008; Rolando & Pacheco, 2005). Hence, it is not just about a re-configuration of the media system designed to adulate the leaders and promote a cult of personality – as it was the case of the Soviet Union under Stalin – but one that rather underpins the notion that the leader is the representation of the collective voice and that the collective voice has a space in the media. One that can, in addition, address all issues and provide strong and steady leadership in the best interests of the people.

Consequently, from the media spaces such as the *Aló Presidente* television program, major decisions were made for national life, and from this same space the symbolic government action was built. President Nicolás Maduro inherited practices and communicational apparatus, but his lack of charisma and improvisation turned some of his messages into mockery and he was never able to connect with the people in the same manner as Hugo Chávez did.

Overall, in the past two decades there has been a clear attempt to create a new communication framework that could provide the Chavismo the ability to exercise ideological hegemony and political power over the country. From the start, this meant to undertake, with great political force, the task of demolishing the old regime hegemonic and ideological structures at all levels (Hernández, 2005, p. 18) and replacing them with new ones that reflected the new order and that aimed at fulfilling the political and cultural aspirations of the Bolivarian Revolution of 1998.

The turning point in the radicalization and acceleration in implementing this new hegemony came in the form of Hugo Chávez Frías' response to the military coup of April 11, 2002 and the following Venezuelan general strike of 2002–03, also known as the oil strike – or oil lockout. These events saw a media alignment with opposition factors, which assume an active role in the world of communications. The *Chavista* regime hit back over the years with a series of measures and policies that translated into a complete overhaul of the media landscape, which included changes in the ownership, new broadcast licensing legislation and arrangements, types of outlets and platform provisions available, and, most importantly, changing the political alignments and loyalties emanating from the existing media outlets.

This new political and legal framework was originally outlined and justified as a public policy against the previous oligopoly and political dominance of the traditional mainstream mass media. In the initial stages it was argued and conceptualized as an effort to promote a public media service. This by changing the ethos and legal framework of the media landscape in the backdrop of constitutional reforms (Cañizález, 2014; Dinneen, 2012). The end product was, however, very different given the existing political tensions and the degree of polarization within the whole period. Soon after, these efforts rapidly became more about counter-information, information warfare, and ideological confrontation with exiting and imaginary enemies of the regime.

One by one, the *Chavista* regime has taken out its opponents in the media sphere. This either by withdrawing broadcasting rights, pressuring cable operates and Internet Service Providers to withdrew channels and outlets from its platforms, using the state repressive apparatus to make people sell, or simply by the incarceration or bribing of journalists and media owners. Taken to an impossible corner, many of the remaining media actors either have left or became subservient to the new powerful regime. The media system today, particularly with regard to the provisions to gather, produce, and disseminate news, is nothing but a shadow of what it was.

In parallel to this, the *Chavista* regime went to develop its own media apparatus that had no pretense of being a public service provider but rather a tool to enhance and support the media and cultural changes to advance the Bolivarian Revolution. This includes ample purges of employees in the existing media outlets and provisions such as *Venpres* (now *Agencia Venezolana de Noticias*), *Corporación Venezolana de Televisión* (VTV), TVes (which took over *RCTV* signal), *Radio Nacional de Venezuela*, a series of local and regional broadcasters such as *Vive TV* and *Avila TV*, and, a daily newspaper, the *Correo del Orinoco*.

Meanwhile, supporters of the *Chavista* regime have been creating their own popular media provisions. Perhaps one of the best known is *Aporrea.org*, which is considered broadly supportive but that shows important spaces for dissidence and criticism toward the regime. This particular network has demonstrated the value of networked news and information among community and grassroots groups (Artz, 2012, 2015). Hence, the development of an entire new media landscape has, sort of, responded to the larger initiative of supporting the revolution. This reflected broadly,

> The strategy of "state for revolution" is a conscious process of building independent working-class institutions with decision-making power and control. This strategy has three interrelated elements that conform to the three components describing state power presented above: in production and ownership; in political power; and in cultural norms. The Chavez government has declared socialism as its goal with workers' control of a nationalised means of production a first step. This is not simply nationalisation and government expropriation of industry. Rather, changing ownership of the means of production includes laws and policies for changing the relations of production through workers' councils, community councils and workers' militias—no government control over production, but worker and community control to decide allocation of resources locally, regionally and nationally.
>
> (Artz, 2012)

Nevertheless, the reality was very different. In the end, the new communicational hegemony ended up being the government-state taking over the media in the ways that traditional dictatorships have always done in the past.

The new *Chavista* hegemony has not completely set aside freedom of the press as it keeps many legal provisions in its normative legal framework that, at least in theory, safeguards these rights. However, since the arrival to power of "Socialism of the 21st Century' project," we find systematic cases of journalists and media outlets that had the need to go to the Inter-American Human Rights System, seeking the protection that Venezuelan justice has denied them until now (Bisbal, 2018; Orlando, 2017). Indeed, it is the case that rulers who want to dominate a society often fear criticism and push to exclude or control the news media that they feel are critical. This is exactly the case of the *Chavismo*, which over the past 20 years has demonstrated its intention to perpetuate itself in power by controlling all the institutions of the country, including the media.

Study after study has confirmed that censorship, for example, has become part of state policy and that the long history of attacks on freedom of expression and information in the country, since Hugo Chávez came to power in 1999, have not been fortuitous but orchestrated (Bermúdez, 2007; Cañizález, 2019; Cañizález & Matos-Smith, 2015). The direct closure of media outlets, the suffocation of the press through the state monopoly in the importation of newspaper, open violence against journalists, the indirect censorship that places on the media the responsibility of suspending certain communicators under threat of sanctions, the use of the judicial system to pressure and twist editorial lines, and the sale of key media outlets – under coercion – to opaque capitals and collaborators have all been happening within the broader context of creating a new power hegemony that is both ideological and culturally prevalent (Cañizález, 2019; Pasquali, 2007).

The *Chavista* regime, however, is not totalitarian in the terms describe by seminal scholars (Arendt, 2017 [1951]; Gregor, 1969). It claims that it provides guarantees for freedom of expression and in many cases it allows degrees of dissidence and criticism to a point. However, while doing so, it encroaches against its media enemies depriving them of resources and access to capital. Slowly but inexorably, for example, newspapers have been dying in Venezuela at an astonishing rate in the sea of a declining economy that have no readers nor advertisers to sustain the traditional political economy of the past.

In what has been described by observers as the "agony" of the printed press, Venezuela saw in less than two years some 67 mainstream newspapers stop printing amid the brutal economic crisis while the remaining ones are at unsustainable levels in terms of circulation and advertisement, according to statistics from the Institute of Press and Society Venezuela (IPYS). Similar numbers indicate that since 2013, over 115 newspapers have permanently shut down and many of its proprietors declare bankruptcy. That is more than 70% of the universe of newspaper before that year.

Not all newspapers and media outlets targeted by the government are critical. The latest to stop circulating in its print version was the daily *Panorama*, which for the past 104 years had been the most widely read and political influential in the west of the country. It just ran out of paper and spare parts for its printing press while highly indebted to its suppliers and vendors as the government, its main ally and sponsor, systematically failed to pay huge debts of the newspaper affecting its ability to cancel debts suppliers and also failed to pay *Panorama* itself for advertisement and other services it owed (Mioli, 2019). Indeed, as Nobel Laureate John Maxwell Coetzee (1996) once wrote, censorship has no ideology. Perhaps no place is this truer than in Venezuela under the *Chavista* regime, where today's allies are tomorrow's foe in a cycle of internal purges and counter-purges.

Hegemony halfway

Over the past 20 years, the *Chavista* regime synthetically created a communication model that has been characterized, among other things, by: (a) a legal architecture to regulate the private media; (b) partisan management of the entities in charge of the official oversight such as the National Telecommunications Commission (Conatel); (c) excessive use of national radio and television networks; (d) the propaganda nature that it gave to the media administered by the state, together with the numerical expansion of the governmental media apparatus. However, in parallel to this, it has literally crushed dissident voices by starving to death independent newspapers, jailing journalists, and sending hordes of followers to attach any news media organization that dares to question its hegemony.

However, in 2015 and despite achieving absolute control of the political institutions, having extended its power over the media and still in hold of very large monetary and gold reserves in the central bank, the *Chavista* regime lost by an overwhelming majority the parliamentarian elections (Cannon & Brown, 2017; Pantoulas & McCoy, 2019). This against all odds, given the rigged electoral system controlled by their key allies, ample support of the armed forces, and the fact that it had sent to jail key members of the opposition while proscribing several political parties.

Its response was to jail more opponents, close more media outlets, and call, just a year later, a phoney election to designate a last-minute made-up National Constitutional Assembly, which arbitrarily annulled most of the decisions made by the democratically elected parliament. Since then, the country has entered on a spiral of chaos that is now aggravated by direct geo-political confrontations of key stakeholders such as the United States, Russia, China, and, of course, Cuba, which has descended in Venezuela with thousands of its key intelligence operators (Demarest, 2018; Ginter, 2013).

This response, however, could not hide the fact that despite imposing a new hegemony and holding power over all the institution of public life, the *Chavismo* had lost the popular vote and, with it, the street support that it once had. It was part of a long decline in popularity in a highly polarized political environment that revealed the shaky grounds of the regime. Faced with the collapsing economy the *"Media Caesarism"* proved to be insufficient to win the hearts and minds of the people, and after 20 years of ideological indoctrination at schools and across all media platforms, the common citizen was still not buying into the empty and bankrupt new model that proves to be far more corrupt and incompetent than the ancient regime of the Fourth Republic. The remaining support to the regime lays on a relatively small percentage of die-hard constituency that keep the illusion of popular support attending sporadic street manifestations in support of Maduro and the regime.

In the end, the cultural and political hegemony that the *Chavismo* has tried to develop over the past two decades resulted in being too dependent upon in its figurehead, Hugo Chávez, and not sustainable without its oil resources. While the regime gasps to remain in power by allowing the destruction of extensive areas of its rainforest in order to sell gold in the black market and allows narco-cartels and guerilla groups to operate almost freely across its territory (Franqui, 2019; Paolini, Felipe, & Sureda, 2017), people struggle to make ends meet. This to the point that over five million have by now left the country in long marches that have taken many of them from Caracas to Buenos Aires by foot. Will the regime survive to this and the US sanctions? Well, it might do so because it still counts with the support of key elements in the army and controls the means of violence, thanks, in part, to Cuban, Iranian and Russian aid, logistics and amilitary support. However, if it manages to stay in power, it will not be because of a hegemonic setting that, from the beginning, had feet of clay.

References

Aguirre, J. M., & Bisbal, M. (1981). *La ideología como mensaje y masaje*. Caracas: Monte Ávila Editores.

Arendt, H. (2017 [1951]). *The origins of totalitarianism*. London: Penguin.

Artz, L. (2012). Venezuela: Making a "state for revolution"–the example of community and public media. *Links International Journal for Socialist Renewal*. Retrieved from http://links.org.au/node/2849

Artz, L. (2015). Media and power for 21st century socialism in Venezuela. In Fuchs, Christian and Vincent Mosco *Marx and the political economy of the media*. Leiden, the Netherlands: Brill. pp. 490–521.

Atwood, R. (2006). Media crackdown: Chavez and censorship. *Georgetown Journal of International Affairs.* 7(1) 25–32.

Bermúdez, E. (2007). Libertad de expresión y hegemonía en Venezuela. De la hegemonía de los medios a la hegemonía del Estado. *Quórum Académico,* 4(2), 42–60.

Bisbal, M. (1994). *La mirada comunicacional.* Caracas: Alfadil Ediciones.

Bisbal, M. (2018). *La comunicación bajo asedio: Balance de 17 años.* Caracas: AB Ediciones.

Cañizález, A. (1991). *Los medios de comunicación social.* Centro Gumilla. Caracas: Centro Gumilla.

Cañizález, A. (2002). *Entre el estruendo y el silencio: La crisis de abril y el derecho a la libertad de expresión e información.* Caracas: Universidad Católica Andrés Bello/Fundación Konrad Adenauer.

Cañizalez, A. (2007). Medios y pluralismo en Venezuela. *Chasqui. Revista Latinoamericana de Comunicación,* No. 98, 4–9.

Cañizález, A. (2014). The state in pursuit of hegemony over the media: The Chávez model. In M. Guerrero & M. Márquez-Ramírez (Eds.), *Media systems and communication policies in Latin America* (pp. 157–77). London: Palgrave Macmillan.

Cañizález, A. (2016). *Hugo Chávez: La presidencia mediática.* Caracas: Editorial Alfa.

Cañizález, A. (2019). *20 años de censura en Venezuela (1999–2018).* Barcelona: Editorial Alfa.

Canizalez, A., & Matos-Smith, M. (2015). The case of globovision and the implementation of mixed-authoritarian model in the media system. *Iberoamericana,* 15(59), 127–40.

Cannon, B., & Brown, J. (2017). Venezuela 2016: The year of living dangerously. *Revista de Ciencia Política,* 37(2), 613–33.

Carosio, A. (2016). Política social en Venezuela. Las misiones sociales. *Revista Entornos,* 29(2), 61–73.

Chehonadskih, M. (2017). The comrades of the past: The soviet enlightenment between negation and affirmation. *Crisis Critique,* 4(2), 87–105.

Coetzee, J. (1996). *Giving offense: Essays on censorship.* Chicago, IL: University of Chicago Press.

Corrales, J. (2015). The authoritarian resurgence: Autocratic legalism in Venezuela. *Journal of Democracy,* 26(2), 37–51.

Demarest, G. (2018). The Cubazuela problem. *Military Review,* 98(6), 50–65.

Dinneen, M. (2012). The chavez government and the battle over the media in venezuela. *Asian Journal of Latin American Studies,* 25(2), 27–53.

Erlich, F. D. (2005). Características y efectos del discurso autocentrado en Aló Presidente. *Boletín de lingüística,* 24, 5–32.

Frajman, E. (2014). Broadcasting populist leadership: Hugo chavez and alo presidente. *Journal of Latin American Studies,* 46(3), 501–26.

Franqui, B. (2019). Destrucción del Arco Minero se replica en Aragua y Carabobo. Retrieved from https://cronica.uno/destruccion-del-arco-minero-se-replica-en-aragua-y-carabobo/

Gates, L. (2010). *Electing Chávez: The business of anti-neoliberal politics in Venezuela*. Pittsburgh, PA: University of Pittsburgh Press.
Ginter, K. (2013). Truth and mirage: The Cuba-Venezuela security and intelligence alliance. *International Journal of Intelligence and CounterIntelligence, 26*(2), 215–40.
Gramsci, A. (2005 [1935]). *Selections from the prison notebooks*. London: Lawrence and Wishart.
Gregor, J. (1969). *Ideology of fascism*. New York: Free Press.
Hepp, A. (2013). *Cultures of mediatization*. Hoboken, NJ: John Wiley & Sons.
Hernández, D. (2005). Profundizar en el debate teórico para demoler la ideología del viejo régimen. *Palabra y Media, 4*(1), 15–20.
Irwin, D., & Micett, I. (2008). *Caudillos, militares y poder: Una historia del pretorianismo en Venezuela*. Caracas: Universidad Católica Andrés Bello.
Jankovic, N., Colin, M. O., Ari, M., & Haidacher, A. (2019). The divided Venezuela. *International Journal of Foresight and Innovation Policy, 14*(1), 5–18.
Knight, B., & Tribin, A. (2019). *Opposition media, state censorship, and political accountability: Evidence from Chavez's Venezuela* (0898–2937). Cambridge, MA. Retrieved from https://www.nber.org/papers/w25916
Lenoe, M. (2004). *Closer to the masses. Stalinist culture, social revolution, and soviet newspapers*. Cambridge, MA: Harvard University Press.
Lim, J. C. (2015). *Leader symbols and personality cult in North Korea: The leader state*. Abingdon, Oxfordshire: Routledge.
López-Maya, M., Calcaño, L., & Maingón, T. (1989). *De punto fijo al pacto social: Desarrollo y hegemonía en Venezuela, 1958–1985*. Caracas: Fondo Editorial Acta Científica Venezolana.
Lugo-Ocando, J. (2007). Modern conflicts in Latin America. In V. Fouskas (Ed.), *The politics of conflict: A survey* (pp. 22–43). Abingdon, Oxfordshire: Routledge.
Lugo-Ocando, J. (2008). *The media in Latin America*. Maidenhead, Berkshire: Open University Press/McGraw-Hill Education.
Lugo-Ocando, J., & Romero, J. (2003). From friends to foes: Venezuela's media goes from consensual space to confrontational actor. *Revista Electrónica Sincronía, 8*(1). http://sincronia.cucsh.udg.mx/lugoromero.htm
Maingon, T. (2016). Política social y régimen de bienestar. Venezuela 1999–2014. *Estudios Latinoamericanos*. No. 38, 115–43.
Mioli, T. (2019). 104-year-old daily is the latest Venezuelan newspaper to stop print edition due to lack of paper. *Journalism in the Americas blog*. Retrieved from https://knightcenter.utexas.edu/blog/00-20880-104-year-old-daily-latest-venezuelan-newspaper-stop-print-edition-due-lack-paper
Mouffe, C. (2014). Hegemony and ideology in Gramsci. In C. Mouffe (Ed.), *Gramsci and Marxist theory* (pp. 178–214). Abingdon, Oxfordshire: Routledge.
Mujica, H, (208 [1982]). *El imperio de la noticia. Algunos problemas de la información en el mundo contemporáneo*. Caracas: AVN.

Naím, M., & Piñango, R. (1986). *El caso Venezuela: Una ilusión de armonía.* Caracas: Ediciones IESA.

Orlando, F. (2017). *Libertad de expresión en Venezuela.* Caracas: Fundación Editorial Jurídico Venezolana.

Pantoulas, D., & McCoy, J. (2019). Venezuela: Un equilibrio inestable. *Revista de ciencia política (Santiago), 39*(2), 391–408.

Paolini, J., Felipe, J. J., & Sureda, B. (2017). Threats to the sustainability of the Venezuelan Guiana watersheds. *Academia Journal of Environmental Science, 5*(6), 102–7.

Parker, D. (2005). Chávez and the search for an alternative to neoliberalism. *Latin American Perspectives, 32*(2), 39–50.

Pasquali, A. (1980). *Comunicación y cultura de masas.* Caracas: Monte Ávila Editores.

Pasquali, A. (2007). La libertad de expresión bajo el régimen chavista: Mayo de 2007. *Signo y Pensamiento, 26*(50), 265–75.

Penfold-Becerra, M. (2007). Clientelism and social funds: Evidence from Chavez's Misiones. *Latin American Politics and Society, 49*(4), 63–84.

Porto, J. (2019). Venezuela: Medios comunitarios, movimientos sociales y Estado. *RevCom, 4*(8), 1–17.

Ramos-Jiménez, A. (1999). Venezuela: El ocaso de una democracia bipartidista. *Nueva Sociedad, 161,* 35.

Rodríguez, P., Morales, J., & Monaldi-Marturet, F. (2012). *Direct distribution of oil revenues in Venezuela: A viable alternative?* Working Paper 306. Washington, DC.: Center for Global Development. https://www.cgdev.org/sites/default/files/1426486_file_Rodriguez_et_al_Venezuela_OTC_FINAL_0.pdf

Rolando, I., & Pacheco, G. (2005). *Estudio de las relaciones civiles militares en Venezuela desde el siglo XIX hasta nuestros días.* Caracas: Universidad Católica Andrés Bello.

Sánchez, R. (2016). *Dancing Jacobins: A Venezuelan genealogy of Latin American populism.* New York: Fordham University Press.

Sotomayor, C. (2019). Poverty and social assistance in Maracay, Venezuela. *Archaeofauna, 36*(72). https://142.4.8.224/index.php/path/article/view/93

Strömbäck, J. (2008). Four phases of mediatization: An analysis of the mediatization of politics. *The International Journal of Press/Politics, 13*(3), 228–46.

Tucker, R. C. (1979). The rise of Stalin's personality cult. *The American Historical Review, 84*(2), 347–66.

Vallenilla Lanz, L., & Harwich-Vallenilla, N. (1991 [1919]). *Cesarismo democrático y otros textos.* Caracas: Fundacion Biblioteca Ayacucho.

Wickham-Crowley, T. P. (1992). *Guerrillas and revolution in Latin America: A comparative study of insurgents and regimes since 1956.* Princeton, NJ: Princeton University Press.

8 Chávez's eyes
An iconic presence in the Venezuelan political communication

Max Römer-Pieretti

Abstract
Political communication in post-Chávez Venezuela has been characterized by a permanent battle between the deceased Chávez's policies of censorship, Nicolás Maduro's rants, and the multifaceted speeches of the opposition.

The omnipresence of Hugo Chávez as guard of the Revolution in the cities' walls is dominant in discourse within political communication in Venezuela, despite his death.

The aim of this analysis is to approach the presence of the deceased Chávez in a semiotic way, as part of the Venezuelan political communication.

Introduction

It is no secret that the political communication of Chavismo uses the commander's eyes to fuel public imagination ever since the electoral campaign of October 2012, the last one in which Chávez participated before dying. Eyes that watch accompany and determine what is "Chavista" and what is not.

Food, transportation, institutions, and streets decorated with their graffiti watch the citizens with those caricatured eyes, similar to the style of Che's face. To be able to understand this Caribbean – and also ubiquitous – political communication demands a semiotics review due to the usage of iconic and iconicity, both for the color red as part of the Bolivarian Revolution and for the use of Chávez's eyes.

From a semiotic point of view, Peirce (1931–58) and Morris (1946) describe the value of the icon and how iconicity is crucial in the communication process. Thus, the criteria used in this review are about the iconic and its iconicity, as well as the power of the iconic in collective imagination (Figure 8.1).

Figure 8.1 Food with the Commander Chávez and President Maduro. Photo by Daniela Pacheco Camilli, not published, January 2020.

Throughout the analysis of the iconicity of Chávez's eyes, we will translate daily life in a series of statements that show the symbolic use of the commander as the reference, existence, and guard of the Revolution.

Theoretical and referential framework

Chávez created a process known as the "Bolivarian Revolution." Although in its early days it did not have that name, over time Chávez and his followers gave the political process this nickname (Martínez & Vaisberg, 2015). The social and political transformation was first revealed with the attempted coup in February 1992, when Chávez, after not being able to meet the objectives that his co-religionists soldiers commissioned him, surrendered to the media leaving in the air a message of responsibility and pause for the power that would be exercised later on. "For now" became the paradigm of those soldiers who, having used red berets in their attempted coup, adopted that color as part of their political identity.

When Chávez was arrested in February 1992, the lieutenant colonel appeared for the first time on TV, surrounded by reporters' microphones. The uniform-clad soldier was subjected to public scorn for him to surrender to the State communications apparatus: the Ministry of Information. Chávez surrendered, yes, he did, but the formulation he used kept resounding like an ethical echo in the minds of many: "For now." With this he attracted armed colleagues, took the blame for the failed coup, but left the message that the social transformation would come when least expected. That image of Chávez with his red beret in front of the microphones was more than enough for Venezuela to turn to idolize him. It was a country tired of political corruption.

Years passed by and Chávez was pardoned and released from prison by President Caldera. As expected, he undertook political activities to seize power, but this time through the ballot boxes.

The 1998 elections gave the military coup a victory. People associated themselves with those words spoken live on television in the wee hours of early February 1992. Although Chávez knew well the impact of his words and the media brought him to the fore for taking ownership of a failure, it was certainly a strategic mistake on the part of the Ministry of Communications of the Carlos Andres Perez administration. The mass media that was later criticized by Chávez converted the commander into the ideal figure that Venezuelans needed. He perfectly evaluated the workings of the media and took advantage of institutional weakness.

Chávez's ideas in that brief television appearance had its substance. It created power and credibility, and granted the new president with the *auctoritas moral* needed to govern and, what is undeniable, to give himself limitless responsibility. Additionally, another presentation contributed to the establishment of the ideal space for the Chavist thought: his inauguration in 1998.

> I swear to God, I swear before my Homeland, I swear in front of my people and over this dying Constitution that I will promote the democratic transformations needed in order for the new Republic to have a Magna Carta suitable to the present times. I swear it.
> (Chávez, 1999 in Analítica, 1999 in Römer, 2014)

Years went by and with them multiple governmental elections, of constituent assembly, and referenda; in brief, legitimations created "ad hoc" for and by the Revolution.

But Chávez did not care to strengthen the sovereignty apparatus or the institutions to help support his political actions. He acted as a soldier and created multiple social operational systems to meet the many concerns of his followers (Chavistas). Those political actions were named "Missions." The political project was not to strengthen the State apparatus but, instead, to transform it into charitable handouts for whoever was loyal to the process of change which was developing week after week in Venezuela. And those changes determined the president's informative agenda. Every Sunday Chávez frenzied up the population in his "Aló, Presidente," a radio and television show that transmitted his explanations about the blessings of the different missions.

Thus, it can be said that the great platform of ideological distribution for Chavismo adopted the name of missions. These took different forms of social, economic, or medical support (Matheus, 2012 in Römer, 2014).

Furthermore, due to the non-existence of institutionalism to support a State plan, the president himself was the figure in which the whole communication process rested. A paternalistic figure, characteristic of a populist – and even teleological – State, with a simple explanation: things happen because they must happen. And, at the same time, things occur because it is the president who has to ensure that the necessary issues are solved. Under that model, he clearly gained strong loyalties (Römer, 2014).

As such, the presence of Chávez in the missions and in Venezuela's political discourse transformed the president into a messianic figure, a representative of truth and justice. As power in Venezuela has always been understood as paternalistic, Chávez enjoyed a teleological advantage. This means that things happen because they must happen. At the same time, under these conditions of credibility and monitoring, Chávez reformed his discourse into something almost supernatural: a political theology in which he was the only totem.

Rodrigo Navarrete illustrated how the population was meant to comprehend Chávez's eyes in a publication after Chávez's death. Here he offers some arguments about the communication from the Presidency. He says:

> In fact, now it appears that Chávez's eyes reflect and return his image to the Venezuelan nation, inwards and outwards of every social sector that carries it. A successful visual campaign of the V Republic political forces from the outset of graphic production has been that one of Chávez's eyes.
> (Navarrete, 2013, p. 54)

And, in fact, it was so. The campaign was a simple platform to remember the commander, stencil him onto walls and also in many other possible forms of manifestation that lead to convert those eyes and his famous signature, the "pig tail," in popularly used icons. It was, in short, a way to immortalize the leader – that man who gave his life for the people and, furthermore, uplifted them.

Journalist Ludmila Vinogradoff reviewed that gaze two years after Chávez's death.

> In order to promote the commander's myth, Maduro's government invited Chavistas to tattoo themselves with Chávez's eyes and signature all free of charge. The majority has chosen to tattoo the 'pig tail' at the nape of the neck, a very discreet place that can be hidden with hair or a high neck. Nevertheless, the most enthusiastic adherents have tattooed "Chávez's eyes" on the buttocks, and only show them off at the beach or in privacy.
>
> (Vinogradoff, 2014)

In her article, Vinogradoff (2014) points out that Chávez knew he was close to death, and that that campaign, those eyes, would give him permanence in time. He could go down in history like Che Guevara did.

Chávez's eyes' icon is exalted. "He looks at us like an *authority*, ethical and moral, because he has consensual authorization from a large sector of society" (Navarrete, 2013, p. 55).

Not only the campaign of Chávez's eyes promotes the creation of that messianic and theological public imaginary of Chávez. The management of yearly campaigns to pass laws, parliaments, and re-elections converted Chávez into a ubiquitous figure. Either on the campaign trail or not, the different regions represented him as the one capable of transforming poverty into wellness, even if it is only from an iconic point of view. The connection between those handouts and the leader in every phase of communication during the 14 years in power was focused on people, the Chavistas, who adored him for that, for being close, for being in the advertising panels at the entrance of every town, road, and city, and being a part of their lives.

But time went by and Chávez's life vanished. Chávez was very sick with cancer and it was a priority in the last campaign to create an icon of the leader, something that could be converted into serigraphies and applied on walls and t-shirts. An icon that represented the pinnacle of the iconicity of the Bolivarian Revolution's leader. An image that, until today, is still present in the distribution of food with his autograph signature, his shape, and his raised fist. Although nowadays, a little distant from the dictator's death, coupled by the heir of the state plan, Nicolás Maduro.

Recalling that way of thinking that Buxo uses when referring to Valle-Inclan in "The Wonderful Lamp," "nothing is as it is but as remembered. Nothing is as it is but as memory evokes" (Buxó, 2016, p. 100). Chavismo built an ideology of the Revolution on the messianic figure of Chávez. A figure built on the basis of altered memory, in an attempt for remembrance to resemble whatever the political process and its co-religionists wanted the image of Hugo Chávez to be: a reflection rooted in the collective imagination, and an icon that would become part of the people's own life.

The intention is to develop, no matter how, a structure of iconicity that goes beyond the own show of the ubiquitous eyes of Chávez. It is about the iconic becoming symbolic: common proposals made daily, as part of the Venezuelan's common parlance.

A communicative management of the political process was supported, like everything else in Venezuela, by the figure of great men of the Revolution. Citizens absorbed those icons embracing them as part of their lives, as part of a communicational conduct in which the Chavist syntagma, the presence of the new Venezuelan political figures, and those leaders are essential.

During the second elections without Chávez, the elections for mayors and councilmen under Maduro's term, the leader of the United Socialist Party of Venezuela (Partido Socialista Unido de Venezuela, PSUV) and the President of the National Assembly by then, Diosdado Cabello, said: "We have used some symbols related with our Commander Chávez, our leader, our master, our brother, our comrade, the guide of this Revolution" (martinoticias.com, 2013). A Cuban's Revolution usage style, with the presence of the "Che" Guevara throughout the whole communication process. The intention is to highlight the omnipresence in the gaze of the eternal commander, or the beret of the other commander, the one who fought together with Fidel Castro, that from the Caribbean island.

Influence and persuasion for manipulation

In addition to the elements that we mentioned about the icon of Chávez's eyes, these eyes have a double power. On one hand, they ensure that the image of Chávez continues to influence the people as part of the collective; on the other hand, they give legitimacy of continuity to Nicolás Maduro, and, therefore, to represent Chávez.

The presence of Chávez's eyes everywhere did not escape from that capacity to influence and persuade. Some international media like the BBC reflected it by portraying the omnipresence of the leader (BBC News, 2014). Leo Ramirez's photographs for the news agency France Press were highlighted by several media, given that Chávez's gaze had become part of the urban landscape in a vigilant or closer presence depending on the icon's reader (Figures 8.2 and 8.3).

Figure 8.2 García, O. (January 24, 2020). *Los ojos de Chávez (not published, via WhatsApp)*. Caracas, Dtto. Capital, Venezuela.

Figure 8.3 Chávez's eye with signature "pig tail." AFP PHOTO/Leo Ramírez. Published in BBC News on March 2014.

Iconic and iconicity

In order to understand the phenomenon of Chávez's eyes from the Peircean semiotic, we should first identify the theory of the icon related to its purpose: similarity found with the represented object. In other words, how reliable the icon of Chávez's eyes really is to the commander's gaze. There are several criteria that explain this phenomenon – (a) the similarity approach: this concept, which necessarily refers to the relation between the icon and the represented object, also includes what is known as iconicity, that is the similarity between abstract relations or homologous structures; (b) the icon's frankness: it is the relation proposed by Peirce as the referential implication of frankness that degrades from a referential object which does not exist; and (c) the pragmatic dimension of similarity: Peirce was ahead of the many critics that his model would receive, so he said "anything within the quality field exists individually, and in the case of the law, it is simply an icon of what it represents and can be used as a symbol" (Peirce, § 3.362, § 4.531, § 2.299).

Lastly, he generated the concept of hypoicons, related to images, diagrams, and metaphors (Peirce, § 2.277).

If we look at it from the semiotic point of view, the measurability of the icon is not so, meaning that Chávez's eyes are idealized for the stencils, given that it is a visual metaphor, thus being referred to as iconicity. The intention is for the eyes to be those of the commander, to be those that in some way straddle the reality of representation and become the symbol of the Revolution.

Chavismo's political communicators knew that, when creating that icon, they would have to build a metaphor around that image. One that would mean the existence of a gaze in walls, t-shirts, and cardboard boxes, and much more than occasional language. The metalanguage of the eyes, of their figure and signature denote a sense of belongingness, of forced devotion. Because behind that look there is little food and very little wellness.

We only need to review the photographs of Venezuela, those that peel off the walls and reflect poverty, to see what Chavismo has done in 21 years in power.

If we go from the iconic to iconicity, Morris (1946) provides the clues to understand this phenomenon. Considering that the icon is a graphic or metaphorical representation of a subject or object, the iconicity is the measurability of this icon. Morris states that the icon is an extension of the properties of its denotation. He extends Peirce's concept and considers the iconicity as debased matter of the icon. But, why? Is it not about the measurability of the iconic symbol? The response comes from Wallis (1975) who says that the iconicity is divided into two extremes: schemata and pleromata. The first one is related to pictograms and diagrams, while the second one, the pleromata, is the characteristic of the representation of objects in detail. If we try to explain Chávez's eyes' icon using Morris' and Wallis' definitions, we go back to the understanding of the icon as a metaphor, as schemata. But from Eco's (1972) point of view, it is one with considerable burden, because he considers the icon as arbitrary since he thinks it is necessary to know the referent in order to allocate iconic characteristics. Therefore, being known for all the discursive field, it is also accepted that Chávez's eyes are a metaphorical icon that somehow watches everything that passes by.

Now what? The analysis of the icon

What emerges from the semiotic theory is certain. A truth well known by the people who manage communications in the Chavista government. They initiated a populist action in a diminished democracy, with weak institutions, and became the driving force for social justice. And, of course, seeking that commander Chávez was present in every action promoted by the missions – a special presence full of demagogy, with arguments for the disadvantaged, the poor people. As they developed the discourse, the multimedia narrative, a need for the substitution of the leader by an icon emerged. The icons lead to the representations of the leader in different formats until they finally created the eyes of the commander, used for the first time – as we said – in the 2013 presidential campaign. From then on, to the citizen's chest, the walls, the markets, and the panels that crown every opening and, from there, to become a part of the social and political imaginary of Venezuela.

Finally, the pragmatic validity of the concept of iconicity takes us back to the measurability of common elements between the object represented and the representamen and depends on the perception of similarities. We can begin with a question. Is it necessary to have an icon quantifiably similar to Chávez's face? The answer is yes, because in this way the purpose of permanence of an ideal leadership in public memory is much stronger. As said before, he becomes omnipresent, as was the character of the Big Brother in "1984," the novel by George Orwell. The society is trapped and docked in a political and social ideal that, in a certain way, does not arrive. But, without it – the collective imaginary – it would not be possible to survive in a society in which "the cost to sanity is submission" (Römer, 2017).

If we could view the necessities of the Venezuelans in Maslow's pyramid of needs, those would all be accompanied by the unsolved hope that Chavismo seeks to maintain.

But it makes no sense to analyze Chávez's eyes without analyzing the context in which they rest. This gaze is only valid from the spaces it occupies – walls, t-shirts, placards, stickers, and cardboard boxes. A presence that goes far beyond the political discourse – an omnipresence related to the own social and economic activity of Venezuelans.

Chávez died in 2013 and the heritage he left on the shoulders of Nicolás Maduro is starting to blur in the collective imaginary. That is why there is a relation of twinning in each and every action of communication: fruits in boxes with the images of the leaders of the Chavista Revolution. It is a way of keeping the commander alive, and a way of showing that the mark he left as legacy continues.

Chávez's touch

A society in which the master's hand is everywhere is a subservient society. A meekness that comes from the manipulation of reality, from the handouts and misery received from the authority. It is highly unlikely that without genuflection in front of power one may be able to eat, or to be documented as a citizen of Venezuela or have access to medical attention or simply be minimally treated as a citizen by the law enforcement or state apparatuses. Thus, each step given by the Bolivarian Revolution must be sheltered by the ideologist of this deed: Hugo Chávez.

Regarding the communicative and semiotic power of an icon like Chávez's eyes, it is important to browse the asymmetry of the issuers – Chávez, Chavismo, Maduro – and the receivers of the messages: the Venezuelan people. Inside that discourse of proximity that Chávez's eyes propose, as well as in every communication campaign that has been launched throughout 21 years of Chavismo, it is also true that the political and social divisions caused and that Chavismo maintained pushes away the other half of Venezuelans.

Whoever is not a Chavista lives questioned, away from the government's handouts and apart from the Orwellian life of social control imposed by Chavismo. The opposition's identity is blurred. It is not possible to have Chávez's eyes in the opposition side. Many leaders have passed by and none has remained able to have a counter campaign of equivalent strength.

So, "the symbolic exchange becomes a political issue, a struggle to occupy spaces of emission/reception and turn into a visible speaker and an audible voice" (Hopenhayn, 2002, p. 1). It generates an asymmetry that, if seen from Greimas' point of view, it would not be possible to maintain the discursive opponents in each side of the semiotic square. It is a communicational hegemony sustained ever since the "For now" and that, in a certain way, has annulled any other type of signical need.

Thus, it is

> the political power itself who is responsible for the creation and entry into circulation of the cultural elements that constitute the cultural and political imaginary in Venezuela. A communicative machinery to build messages on the basis of its own symbolic needs, aver the construction of an identity to the measure of the own cultural transformations that are developing in the public and civic space.
>
> (Römer, 2014, p. 61)

When he died, Chávez became the ideal image, a part of the collective imaginary. A figure of essential existence for life in community, for the exercise of living in a collective that, as a zombie, attends behind a portrait seeking for their hunger to be satisfied by Chávez's touch. A person would say to herself: the image of Chávez is a gesture of closeness and proximity, of understanding of my problems and my concerns. An indispensable relationship so they do not forget me for being as part of the Revolution's gear.

But Chávez's eyes bleed and warn Maduro

The situation is not under control in times of Maduro. He has neither the same communicational power nor the presence that the commander had. In this respect, when communicational presence is high, it becomes a part of the landscape and is lost in its own capacity of representation. In Maduro's case, who has followed Chávez's shameful criteria to stay in power, when this pressure over the citizen is exerted on a daily basis, it is deformed as part of the relations with power. But, when pressure coming from the state's security forces toward society is so big, people are capable of doing things that all of the sudden contain what supposedly belongs to the collective imaginary (Figure 8.4).

When the state's security forces, those that are supposed to support and protect the people, shoot them, wound them, and convert them into human debris, people create new imaginaries.

This happened when the National Guard shot student Rufo Chacon, permanently blinding him.

Then Chávez's eyes bled; they cried as the people cried. They cried of indignation, anger, and discontent. In that moment, the iconicity of the Revolution's leader disappeared and became a symbol of fight, protest, and a boomerang against Maduro's regime.

It was as if, all of a sudden, people said to the leaders: you watch me with Chávez's eyes and want his eyes to look at me from everywhere.

Figure 8.4 Oh, Nicolás! I see devaluation. Photo from Ludmila Vinogradoff published in ABC on August 2014.

But that look could be mine, the one that can remain without sight. The same one that you, so powerful, are able to blind. A manipulation of the image that, also from the symbolic, wants to tell Maduro that Chávez is not that one who shoots; he is the one who cries along with his people.

But that which had put Chávez in power and had become part of the collective imaginary, those ubiquitous eyes that dominated everything, became a symbol of protest and became a semiotic argument from the iconicity itself into the most bitter way of emphasizing that it was enough.

It did not take much more to understand that power was transferred from the authorities to the people with bloody eyes. There was no need for the political power to impose a way of doing and seeing things. The icon's strength was transmuted and became a legisignic-symbolic-argumentative relationship, the maximum exponent of the Peircian sign – a sign that makes its semiosis in syllogism.

A syllogism which is expressed in a way similar to this: if Chávez is his people and his eyes watch us, then when people are wounded or killed by the power itself, Chávez's eyes cry tears of blood as the people do.

Chávez's gaze in everyday life

We mentioned George Orwell and his novel "1984." We have seen how the Big Brother is the most frightening character of the society that the British author describes in its pages. Whoever finds their way into the pages of the novel ends up being terrified, assuming that the way of life described should be far from reality. And as fiction, it is only that: words that happen and imagine a world of shame and terror. What an expert reader of English literature cannot imagine is that that world of tracking, hunger, and violence exists. Neither can she imagine the possibility of a country living together with the leader and ideologist of a crushing and suffocating society, such as the one of the Chavista socialism of the 21st century. And, on top of that, to have to bear that the eyes of its ideologist are capable of staying alive by the work and grace of serigraphy and stencil, well after his death.

References

BBC News. (5 de marzo de 2014). En fotos: la omnipresencia de los ojos de Hugo Chávez. *BBC News*. Retrieved from: https://www.bbc.com/mundo/video_fotos/2014/03/140305_galeria_fotos_chavez_ojos_venezuela_vh. [13-12-2020]

Buxó, M. J. (2016). *Tecnopaisajes, identidades y diseños culturales*. Barcelona: Universidad de Barcelona.

Eco, U. (1972). Introduction to a semiotics of icons signs. *Versus 2*, pp. 1–15.

Hopenhayn, M. (2002) El reto de las identidades y la multiculturalidad. *Pensar Iberoamérica: Revista de Cultura (0)*. Retrieved from: http://www.almamater.edu.co/Servicios/Integracion_Academica/Diplomado_Cultura_Democratica/Sesiones/Sesion_09/El_reto_de_las_identidades_y_la_multiculturalidad%20-%20Martin_Hopenhayn.pdf. [13-12-2020]

Martínez, M., &. Vaisberg, R. (2015). La narrativa revolucionaria del chavismo. *PostData, 19(2)*, 463–506.

martinoticias.com. (3 de septiembre de 2013). Venezolanos votarán bajo "la mirada de Chávez." *Radio Televisión Martí*. Retrieved from: https://www.radiotelevisionmarti.com/a/comicios-municipales-venezuela-diciembre2013-alcaldes-concejales-/27070.html [10–02–2020]

Morris, C. (1946 [1971]). Signs, language and behavior. In C. Morris, *Writings on the general theory of signs* (pp. 73–398). Mouton: La Hague.

Navarrete, R. (2013). Los ojos de Chávez. In E. Cobos, *Rostros y rastros de un líder: Hugo Chávez. Memoria de un pueblo* (pp. 54–75). Caracas: Centro Nacional de Historia y Servicio Autónomo Imprenta Nacional y Gaceta Oficial.

Orwell, G. (1949 [2017]). *1984*. Barcelona: Penguin Random House Grupo Editorial.

Pacheco-Camilli, D. (20 de enero de 2020). *Aguacates con Chávez y Maduro – fotografías (not published, via WhatsApp)*. Caracas, Dtto. Capital, Venezuela.

Peirce, C. (1931–1958). *Collected papers*. Vols. 1–6. ed. Hartshorne, Charles, and Weiss, Paul; vols. 7–8 ed. Burks, Arthur W. Cambridge, MA: Harvard University Press.

Römer, M. (2014). Venezuela a partir de Chávez: identidad cultural y política. *Historia y Comunicación Social, 19(esp.)*, 55–65.

Römer, M. (16 de agosto de 2017). El precio de la cordura es la sumisión. Eldebatedehoy en. https://eldebatedehoy.es/politica/hermano-mayor-orwell/ [13-12-2020]

Vinogradoff, L. (10 de agosto de 2014). La mirada de Chávez. *ABC Blogs*, págs. https://abcblogs.abc.es/bochinche-venezolano/sociedad/la-mirada-de-chavez.html [13-12-2020]

Wallis, M. (1975). *Arts and signs*. Bloomington: Indiana Press University.

9 Between resistance and reinvention

Cultural diffusion in Venezuelan media

Moraima Guanipa

Abstract
This chapter explores how information about culture has been presented in the Venezuelan media within the context of the complex transformations that have taken place, both in cultural institutions and in the national mediascape. During this period, government actions have been oriented to the centralization, oversight, and attempted exercise of control of cultural activities. However, this period has also seen the emergence of some private initiatives which foster greater plurality. Cultural journalism has evidenced these transformations from the media perspective that have also suffered the economic crisis, censorship, and technological changes resulting in huge losses of readership.

Introduction

Declining diversity in the media has become a defining feature of the late 20th-century Venezuelan journalism, as evidenced by the decreasing coverage about culture, now mostly covered only as mere event listings. Examining its main landmarks during the past two decades requires identifying some of the characteristics of the information processes around changing and challenging cultural and communicational dynamics. This analysis details some of these transformations while engaging in a brief discussion about the roles communication and culture play in current societies, as well as the contexts in which these sectors became targeted by the Venezuelan government, greatly impacting journalistic endeavors around cultural information.

Cultural journalism: from high culture to media culture

In Latin America, Aníbal Ford's definition of culture as a "form of meaning-making, as a reading of quotidian life, as mediation"

(Rivera, 2003, p. 178) is imprecise. García Canclini (1989, 1999) says it best, stressing the hybrid character of Latin American modernity, which demands a multi-tiered vision of culture as a series of watertight and waterproof compartments of the cultured, the massive, and the popular. Similarly, Martín Barbero (1991) argues that much of the population in Latin America has concentrated on the adoption of the values of the Enlightenment, as evidenced in the media, in cultural industries, and in the context of urban cultures.

Linked from its origins to the Enlightenment, the written culture of newspapers and print media represents a crucial chapter in the history of journalism and culture. Such media contributed to the modern idea of the nation, the "imagined communities" Anderson (1993) referenced and whose "print capitalism" spearheaded the production of national consciousness.

Newspapers derive their importance not only from their longevity among mass media, but from the privileged place they occupy in constantly updating public opinion and in providing journalistic information. As Olga Dragnic (1993) emphasized, "historically, information about arts and literature first emerged and developed, but progressively it became displaced by the power of the massive and the cultural industry, which required the corresponding information space" (p. 36). Coverage of culture and its expressions gained autonomy and space, while professionalization and specialization of journalists followed soon thereafter. Several generations of reporters provided daily information about different cultural topics and their specific sources: literature, fine arts, music, theater, and dance, among others.

As Venezuela's cultural institutional fabric expanded during the latter half of the 20th century, brought about by modernization and spurred by an oil bonanza, culture gained more centrality in media. This prompted the emergence of arts and culture sections across media, both in Caracas and in the regions.

Media, communication, and hegemony: contextual elements

From the beginning, Hugo Chávez's project sought to institutionally disarticulate media and culture as key areas in the construction of imaginaries and public opinion. Safar (2013) argues that the country's institutional and legal fabric transformational process began in 1999 with the Constitution, enacting a series of changes to its legal framework and creating several new institutions.

The displacement of managers and agents in cultural institutions in 2001 under the "Bolivarian Cultural Revolution" was discursively justified as a renewal of the bureaucratic cadres occupied by a presumed "elite," bringing about what Silva-Ferrer (2017) called vacating the cultural institutions. Instead of prompting their democratization, this imposed "the widening and increased sophistication of the control and disciplinary device of culture and communication" (p. 37). Various authors (Kozak, 2015; Centeno and Mata, 2017; Ramos, 2019) have stressed the Gramscian undergirding of the chavista project in the "construction of a new communicational hegemony" (Kozak, 2015, p. 52), as Hugo Chávez's former minister of Communication and Information, Andrés Izarra, advanced in 2007 (Weffer, 2007). This implied dismantling the symbolic and ideological universes, as Gramsci had conceived. The transformation of culture would follow, as hegemony "should not be understood merely in formal political terms, but rather as a cultural issue, since it implies the imposition of an entire worldview" (Centeno and Mata, 2017, p. 38). This institutional scaffolding was spearheaded by the creation of the Ministry of Popular Power for Culture and several connected initiatives in 2005, substituting the three-decade-old Conac.

Silva-Ferrer has focused on the social effects of this hegemonic impulse to control and monopolize the public sphere in Venezuela, which he asserts spurred a migration of culture toward the private sphere, a survival and resistance strategy of cultural agents seeking to escape "from the disciplinary domain that was being imposed as part of the State's policies" (2013, p. 284). This prompted the emergence of private initiatives that mobilized publics, revitalized cultural consumption, and opened the institutional spectrum toward theaters, cinemas, visual arts expositions, and bookstores in new cultural centers such as Hacienda La Trinidad, Trasnocho Cultural, and the Centro de Artes Los Galpones, among others.

The press: between highbrow culture and the massive industrial

Print media lay testament to the dramatic transformations in the Venezuelan mediascape throughout these two decades. In addition to the changes in the information agendas and foci of the media themselves, print media pagination suffered from the growing economic limitations, advertising and readership declines, and the lack of access to foreign currency for acquiring newsprint and other necessary supplies. This was compounded by the unrelenting wave of digitization and the growth of old and new outlets on the Web and social media.

In a research project on ten years of Venezuelan press (1999–2008), I looked at *El Universal* (1909) and *El Nacional* (1943) – two of the most significant national newspapers with greater tradition in covering culture – offering clues to comprehend some of the characteristics of the approach toward culture in Venezuelan press during this time, which are still present.

Both media diversified and went beyond the fine arts and highbrow or elitist culture. However, their migration toward cultural industries and the commercial logic that undergirds them, beyond widening the field, also implied trivializing and spectacularizing the culture pages, as evidenced in the selection of topics and the privileging of superficial and ephemeral treatments. Similarly, they risked a low quality of information in the texts, as noted in the multiplicity of messages with few or no sources or bylines (see graphs 1 and 2).

El Nacional, in particular, "was the open stage for writers and intellectuals to communicate to the country" (Pulido, 2019). These guiding spaces, with their consecrating and polemicizing, have all but disappeared from print media or, at best, have become circumscribed to literary or cultural supplements (Figure 9.1).

This data, from two of the most influential Venezuelan media outlets, former beacons in approaching cultural contents, shows how print cultural journalism has favored shorter copy without attribution

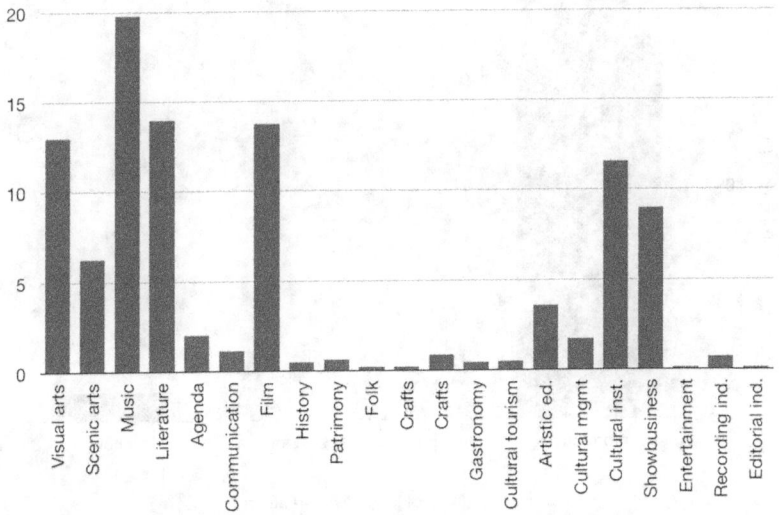

Figure 9.1 Theme areas in cultural press expressed as percentages (1998–2008). Total content units analyzed: 1.391.
Source: Author.

or byline. Similarly, it shows how coverage of showbusiness and entertainment has eclipsed that of music in all forms, underlining a shift toward the notion of entertainment as the main referent that englobes all of culture (Figure 9.2).

These tendencies are further strengthened by demands to adjust the space devoted to news, within a complex context for the Venezuelan press. Several newspapers, *El Nacional* among them, have ceased to print either temporarily or definitively, as noted in reports by IPYS-Venezuela and Prodavinci (2018) and Espacio Público (2018).

Contributing factors to this are the country's political and economic conditions of the past decade, the persecution of independent media, and the lack of access to newsprint and supplies initially caused by their exclusion as priority imports since 2012 and, later, by the monopolistic actions of the Complejo Editorial Maneiro. *El Universal*, however, was part of an unusual process of change in ownership of several Venezuelan outlets over the past decade, establishing

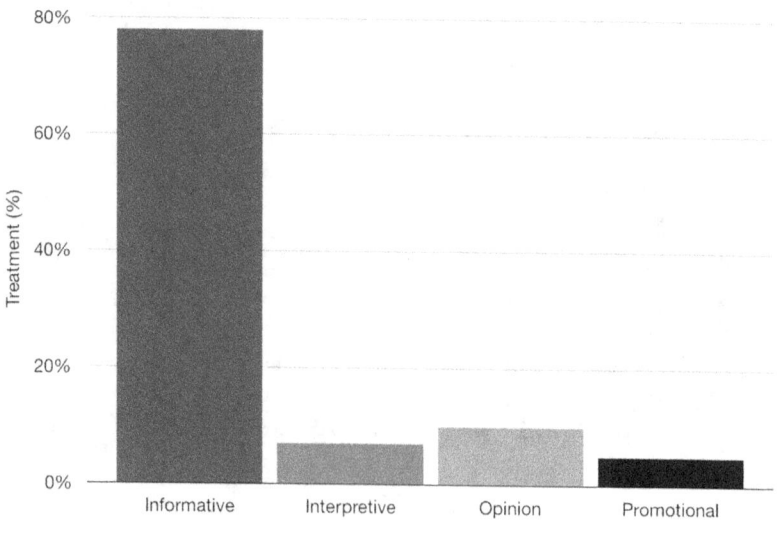

Figure 9.2 Journalistic treatments expressed as percentages. Total content units analyzed: 1.391.
Source: Author.

what Carmen Beatriz Fernández has called the "new communicational architecture" (2014).

Most regional media had reporters covering this beat, as did three newspapers no longer in print – Barquisimeto's *El Impulso*, Marcaibo's *Panorama*, and Valencia's *El Carabobeño*. Regional newspapers, which represented 51% of the national press in the 1980s (Quiñones, 2008, p. 88), also felt the country's severe political and economic crisis of the past two decades. Although some of them migrated and persist in the digisphere, others ceased print and announced either temporary or definitive closures, causing newspaper deserts in at least three states (Espacio Público, 2018).

Death and reinvention of media

In the late 20th century, Julio Miranda (1996) observed that "the reduction in magazines has led to a reduction in the spaces for critique, which had already suffered in the culture pages and literary supplements in the press" (p. 236). This phenomenon has only increased since.

Supplements such as *Últimas Noticias*'s "Cultura," *El Universal*'s *Verbigracia*, and the literary pages of regional media such as Barquisimeto's *El Impulso* were spaces for diffusion and debate around culture and literature in Venezuela and abroad. Some of these would cease circulation following editorial decisions and, others, the aforementioned reduced pagination.

Others would reinvent themselves, attending to the communicational and media consumption realities marked by the Internet, listservs, social media and mobile apps, such as WhatsApp. Along the way, other longstanding publications withered. For example, the impeccably edited *Bigott* magazine, sponsored by the namesake foundation and tobacco corporation, which since 1981 had covered topics from highbrow culture to folklore and handcrafts and which, in 2004, was replaced, albeit shortly, by *Veintiuno* magazine.

The lack of culture in electronic media

Throughout the past two decades, the few spaces providing information on culture on television and radio have nearly vanished, except for a few and notorious exceptions, such as *Los Pasos Perdidos* or *Librería Sónica*. Others have followed the global phenomenon among media such as television, limiting their coverage to showbusiness and entertainment, including gossip, commercial cinema, and international music.

National radio and television, far from opening spaces to enrich the audiences' information diets, have reinforced the levity of the cultural area, in many cases prompting silencing by removing journalistic spaces devoted to information or opinion. In the balance of these two decades lies the disappearance of radio and television stations due to the extinguishing or non-renewal of state licenses (such as RCTV's in 2007), financial and judicial measures, and even physical attacks against their headquarters.

The disappearance of *Emisora Cultural de Caracas* in 2013, the country's first frequency modulation station, is an illustrative exemplar. For ten years, since its founding in 1975, this was Venezuela's sole FM station, broadcasting an overtly cultural content, with a novel patronage scheme that avoided relying on advertisement revenue. Greatly characterized by musical programming heavy on academic music, it aired shows on literature, the arts, and history. "The cultural of Caracas," as it was known, underwent a change in ownership in 2004, and, nine years later, a reassignment of its frequency to a different call sign.

The Caracas Athenaeum radio had a similar cultural approach, broadcasting from 2003 until 2012, when it changed its call sign to *VenFM*. Its programming remained focused on several cultural topics, with some shows produced by journalists and other personalities of Venezuela's cultural areas. This station was one of the many Caracas Athenaeum initiatives, one of the country's most relevant cultural institutions and whose reach extended across the country, articulating a powerful network of regional athenea. Following the termination of its loan in 2009, President Chávez announced its eviction from the building that had housed the institution for more than 25 years, reassigning the space to the nascent Experimental University of the Arts. A significant outlier is *Vale TV*, created in 1998 before the end of Rafael Caldera's second term, by granting the Caracas Archdiocese control over the country's oldest television station, Canal 5 (1952). To this day, *Vale TV* maintains an entirely educational and cultural programming based on documentaries, reportages, and special programs produced externally or in-house.

Cultural information in public media

When Hugo Chávez rose to power, the Venezuelan State had but a meager presence in the national media universe. From just one State-owned and -operated television station, *Venezolana de Televisión*, to a handful of radio stations such as the information and classical music channels of *Radio Nacional de Venezuela*, the government quickly advanced in the construction of a new and mighty communication axis for the dissemination of cultural, educational, and ideological contents. According to Bisbal (2018), following the 2002 coup and the 2002–03 oil strike,

> the government began designing and putting together a media structure without precedent neither in the country nor in Latin America, governmentalized and at the service of the Bolivarian Revolution and the development and implantation of socialism of the 21st century.

Thus, during the 2000s, the government set off configuring a system of public media, currently overseen by the Ministry of Communication and Information (MINCI), known since 2013 as the Bolivarian System of Communication and Information (SIBCI). Considerations for its creation via Executive Order note that "it is without delay that the communicational hegemony must continue to be built." The SIBCI substituted the National Public Media System and its organization brought together media overseen by the Ministry of Communication and Information as well as all other information bodies of the Venezuelan State.

An analysis of the different online portals, social media, and programming schedules of public television stations shows that cultural content is concentrated in *ViveTV* and in some shows on *Telesur* and *ÁvilaTV*. The latter is a station created by the Office of the Mayor of Caracas that focused on urban culture but taken over by the MINCI in 2008. This station also hosts the School of Media and Audiovisual Production, EMPA.

Likewise, the reach of government messaging also expanded in radio, following the diversification of the state-run *Radio Nacional de Venezuela*, as it multiplied its channels to include Classical, Musical, Indigenous, Youth, and International while increasing its outlets in the different regions of the country. Additionally, *YVKE Mundial* AM and FM radio circuit and *La Radio del Sur* broadcast internationally and via Web. A local station, *Alba Ciudad*, offers cultural programming that includes a newscast and shows on different artistic expressions, in addition to productions carried out by this area's public institutions.

Print media were also part of this reconfiguration. For example, in 2009, Chávez promoted the foundation of the *Correo del Orinoco*, namesake to the newspaper founded by Simón Bolívar in 1818. In a clear reference to this connection, the newspaper quoted the Liberator in its motto, who called the printing press "the artillery of thought." This newspaper's print and online editions host a "Communication and culture" page, containing information about public cultural institutions, as well as news about national and international artistic figures, much in line with the editorial framework of a state-run publication.

Notably, this newspaper includes a series of supplements from the Massive Magazine System (*Sistema Masivo de Revistas*), created in 2011 and currently overseen by the Ministry for Culture: *A Plena Voz, Así Somos, Memorias de Venezuela, Se Mueve, La Roca de Crear, La Revuelta*, and *Poder Vivir*. These magazines have become specialized in the government's cultural platforms: scenic and musical arts, cinema, literature, thought, patrimony, and memory.

Another SIBCI publication, *CiudadCcs*, self-identifies as "a Venezuelan newspaper of Chavista ideology." This newspaper was founded in 2009 during the mayoral administration of Jorge Rodríguez, former VP and current Minister of Information. The publication, which includes a culture section focused on the urban and popular arts expressions, is presumably being replicated in other Venezuelan cities.

During the period herein covered, we must also note media directly controlled by the Ministry of Culture, such as *Todos Adentro*. Similarly, *Semanario Cultural de Venezuela*, a free publication founded in 2005, currently circulates as a supplement to *El Correo del Orinoco*, with radio and television versions as well.

Although democratization of the radioelectric spectrum traditionally dominated by private interests should allow greater plurality of voices while incorporating coverage of culture produced on a local and communitarian level, it derived in media that were economically and operationally dependent on the administration. Urribarrí (2013) notes that, in Venezuela, one cannot consider the so-called communitarian media as such. Rather than emerging from the third sector or from NGOs, these media are operated by some community councils, becoming pro-government social organizations and positioning themselves as "an arm of the State-party-government, which is organized and articulated by the central administration." In short, "In the transit from the 20th to the 21st century, *comm*unitarian media became *gov*unitarian" (Urribarrí, 2013, p. 69).

Reinvention online

Shortly after the Web became publicly available and before its expansion into a global phenomenon, in 1996, Jorge Gómez Jiménez launched *Letralia, Tierra de Letras,* Venezuela's first cultural Web publication, devoted to literature. Eight years later, María Antonieta Flores launched *El Cautivo*, a digital poetry magazine that also addressed arts and culture.

Notwithstanding, during the late 20th century, journalists or media managers began developing new digital native media, many of them well received by users craving information. It was journalism's answer to censorship, pressures, closures, and reduction in advertisement and readership.

The irruption of these new digital media ventures was positively perceived in the languishing national mediascape (Cañizález, 2014), as an "unexpected collateral effect" of the restrictions and pressures affecting traditional media: "in the country, several initiatives have flourished, which are led by groups of journalists that seek on the Web a space of independence in an informational system in crisis" (Paone, 2015).

Sembramedia, a nonprofit organization that seeks to increase the diversity of voices and to foster Ibero-American digital entrepreneurship, compiles a Digital Media Directory. To be included in their database, media must meet several criteria: digital native, original content, journalistic and public service orientation, editorially and financially independent of state institutions or political organizations, and not beholden to corporate or donor interests. After reviewing 62 entries for Venezuelan media, I identified ten general interest sites that contained culture and entertainment sections framed within their own information profiles (Table 9.1).

Most of these media use various journalistic genres and treatments, regarding both information and opinion. With varying emphasis, they too conceive cultural events as entertainment. Their coverage includes cinema, multiple expressions of music (particularly those of the recording industry), showbusiness, entertainment, literary news, award ceremonies and artist recognitions, and Venezuelan writers both at home and abroad.

Venezuela's digital universe also hosts multiple publications devoted to cultural content, with offerings focused on the arts and cultural manifestations. These new digital cultural media include an array of information and opinion options, from specialized sites to miscellaneous magazines focusing on the arts and scholarly approximations or initiatives promoting pop culture and rock, such as *Esfera Cultural*, *Tráfico Visual*, *El-Teatro*, and *Cresta Metálica*, among others.

However, digital media have also suffered the adverse economic climate and the closure of financing sources, significantly impacting their business models. This has forced halting the publication of websites such as pop culture-focused *Cochino Pop* or *Revista OJO*, focused on journalistic and literary content.

Table 9.1 Native digital (general scope) media with cultural sections

Outlet	URL	Founded on	Sections
Analítica	https://www.analitica.com/	2004 Information site since 2012	National news, Economy, Crime, World news, Sports, Editorial, Opinion, Regional information, Entertainment (*), Lifestyle, Health, and Well-being (*) In the entertainment section: Showbusiness, Music, Culture, and Cinema
Prodavinci	https://prodavinci.com/	2005 Blog site since 2010	Life, Prodavinci specials, Perspectives, Newsworthy, Latest news, Literature, Arts, Analysis, Chronicle, Sports, Science and technology, Business and economy, Interview
La Patilla	https://www.lapatilla.com/	2010	National news, World news, Opinion, Economy, Politics, Sports, Entertainment, Health, Curiosities, Tourism, La Patilla TV
Guayoyo en letras	http://guayoyoenletras.net/		Editorial, Politics, Social (*), Economy, Interviews, The 7 arts (focused on cinema, chronicles, critique, and storytelling), Technology, Blog, More Guayoyo (*) In the Social section, Guarapita Cultural presents news and information on culture and entertainment.
Contrapunto	https://contrapunto.com/	2014	National news, Economy, Sports, Life, Technology, Arts and entertainment, Global, CTP Interviews, What's new, CTP World Arts and entertainment: Cultural agenda, Visual arts, Cinema, Journalism and communication, Dance, Interview, Events, Photography, Cultural management, Literature, Fashion, Music, Patrimony, People, Polemics, Theater, Traditions and patrimony, TV
El Estímulo	http://elestimulo.com/		Opinion, World news, Sports, Culture, Showbusiness, Venezuela
Caraota Digital	http://www.caraotadigital.net/		National news, World news, Technology, Sports, Entertainment, Caraota Tips

El Pitazo	https://elpitazo.net/	2015	Crime, Politics, Economy, World news, Migration, Health, Opinion, Entertainment (*) Entertainment groups culture and sports. "All of the relevant cultural news and events in Venezuela and abroad."
Efecto Cocuyo	http://efectococuyo.com/		The most recent, Politics, Economy, Mankind (*), Health, Crime, Blogs, Opinion (*) In the Mankind section, there are often contents in reference to what is happening in the cultural and urban realms. This medium also offers an agenda of cultural events
Crónica Uno	http://cronica.uno/		Community (*), Crimes, Economy, Politics, National news, Sports, Specials (*) Community includes a Public Zone section, which contains cultural information

Source: Author, with data from the Sembramedia Digital Media Directory for Venezuela.

The possibility of enduring in time and mustering the needed financial resources is hindered by a 59% Internet penetration in the country (*Informe Estadístico: Cifras del sector – Segundo trimestre de 2019*, 2019), greatly limiting digital media's reach and consumption. As foreseen by Andrés Cañizález, digital media

> ...will continue to have the notable handicap of not reaching half of the country's population to which contrasting information should reach, since it is the half of the country that is disconnected, which is not in densely populated urban areas, and which still uses OTA television as its main – and, sometimes, only – source for news (2014).

The country's low connection speeds, among the slowest in the region (Chirinos, 2019) and among the worst in the world (The global state of digital, 2019), are another obstacle in journalism's use of digital platforms and the Internet, which are compounded by the ongoing electrical supply problems. Just as relevant are blockades and selective DDoS attacks which frequently target some independent outlets, denying access to these media's sites (IPYS, 2019; Espacio Público, 2020).

Resistance and reinvention

This analysis of these past two decades of cultural journalism encapsulates the approach to culture within the sociopolitical framework of the so-called Bolivarian Revolution.

Throughout this time, some media initiatives of obstinate resistance stand out, despite the government's implementation of the "Socialism of the 21st century" model, its discretional use of resources from the country's oil bonanza (1999–2014), and its application of hegemonically aspiring cultural and communicational policies (Kozak, 2015; Delgado Flores, 2008, 2013; Bisbal, 2015). New private institutions and projects emerged in areas ranging from poetry to music, following the closure of spaces and changes to the dynamics of culture. The resistance and reinvention of traditional media and the experiences of new native digital media for a society starving for verified information push against the gradual disappearance of cultural media and sections.

In private media, the sections that focused on cultural activities suffered the pruning of spaces in print and radioelectric media in the county, as well as the departure of journalists, either to migrate or to join other areas of the media market. Some of the most relevant privately owned national newspapers with cultural sections withered to a few pages or, at best, migrated toward digital.

The native digital media that have emerged over the last decade maintain a varied offer of the multiple expressions of cultural information. Although this seemed to herald a widening of themes, agendas, and perspectives, the tendency has been to maintain showbusiness and entertainment as their main referents.

A worrisome lack of coverage, analysis, and interpretation can be noted around the complex processes that make up the value chain of the creation, production, diffusion, promotion/exposition, and consumption/participation (UNESCO, 2009) of the various and growing spaces of cultural and creative industries of our times.

Digital media – far from taking advantage of the possibilities inherent to the virtual spaces, their multimedia nature, and the freedom to overcome the time and space constraints of media such as print, radio, and television – have replicated the brevity and consequent shallowness in their messaging. They, too, homogenize culture and showbusiness, while tending toward the notion of entertainment. Similar moves can be evidenced in Venezuelan radio and television, underlining the notions developed by authors such as Martini (2000) and Kovach and Rosenstiel (2004). Within the context of "infotainment," information subsides to spectacularization and journalism renounces its values, its anchorage in reality, and its elements of competitive advantage: "How could information compete with entertainment if the conditions are set by the latter?" Kovach and Rosenstiel (p. 211) aptly ask.

Faced with the cultural isolation caused by the economic crisis and the government-imposed restrictions hindering the import of books, records, and other cultural products, Venezuela's cultural journalism faces the challenge to generate relevant and quality information. Hence, the importance for journalistic messages and coverage to go beyond the novelties and information from international sources and to explore the potential of the country's remaining cultural and aesthetic creation and production. It is the task of journalists and media alike to diversify the agenda and open spaces for debating globalization and the new cultural citizenships of our times.

References

Anderson, B. (1993). *Comunidades imaginadas. Reflexiones sobre el origen y la difusión del nacionalismo.* México: Fondo de Cultura Econó mica.

Bisbal, M. (2015). Medios de comunicación social en Venezuela. Notas sobre nuestro escenario comunicativo. In Bisbal, M. y Aguirre, J. M. (Eds.), *Encrucijadas de la comunicación en Venezuela.* Caracas: Centro Gumilla y Bid&co, pp. 10–32.

——— (June 26, 2018). Contra la censura. *Prodavinci*. Retrieved June 28, 2018, from https://prodavinci.com/contra-la-censura/
Cañizález, A. (June 10, 2014). Tres fracturas del periodismo venezolano. *El Nacional*. Retrieved June 10, 2014, from http://www.el-nacional.com/opinion/fracturas-periodismo-venezolano_0_424757627.html [10–6–2014].
Centeno Maldonado, J. C., & Mata Quintero, G. (2017). Hegemonía comunicacional y libertad de expresión en Venezuela. El caso RCTV. *Revista Mexicana de Opinión Pública*, 22, 35–53 January–June.
Chirinos, M. (May 25, 2019). Venezuela, Internet al mínimo. *Prodavinci*. Retrieved May 25, 2019, from https://prodavinci.com/venezuela-internet-al-minimo/
Delgado Flores, C. (2008). Políticas culturales en la administración Chávez. El espectáculo de las miserias." *Revista Sic*, Año LXXXI (710), 500–3.
——— (2013). Golpes a la cultura y la comunicación. In Bisbal, M. (Ed.), *Saldo en Rojo. Comunicaciones y cultura en la Era Bolivariana*. Caracas: Universidad Católica Andrés Bello-Konrad Adenauer Stiftung, pp. 259–73.
Dragnic, O. (1993). La cultura mediatizada. *Comunicación: Estudios venezolanos de comunicación*, 19 (81), 34–41.
Espacio Público. (August 7, 2018). La agonía de los periódicos en Venezuela. Retrieved August 18, 2018, from http://espaciopublico.ong/la-agonia-de-los-periodicos-en-venezuela/
Espacio Público. (April 29, 2020). Informe: Situación general del derecho a la libertad de Expresión en Venezuela. Retrieved May 1, 2020, from http://espaciopublico.ong/informe-2019-situacion-general-del-derecho-a-la-libertad-de-expresion-en-venezuela/
García Canclini, N. (1989). *Culturas híbridas. Estrategias para entrar y salir de la modernidad*. México: Grijalbo.
——— (1999). *La globalización imaginada*. Barcelona: Paidós.
Guanipa, M. (2011). Eso que la prensa llama cultura. Análisis de la información cultural en dos medios nacionales." In Arcila, C. and Calderín, M. (Eds.), *Avances de la investigación de la comunicación en Venezuela*. Colección Monografías (Grupo de Investigación Comunicación, Cultura y Sociedad). Asociación de Investigadores Venezolanos de la Comunicación (Invecom), pp. 10–19. http://www.saber.ula.ve/handle/123456789/34311
——— (2013). La agenda de la cultura en la prensa. Análisis temático en dos medios nacionales (1998–2008). *Revista Venezolana de Economía y Ciencias Sociales*. 18 (3), (September-December). Caracas: UCV. 125–38.
——— (2014). La cultura en la prensa: un rostro breve, misceláneo y espectacular. En: Revista *Comunicación. Estudios venezolanos de Comunicación*. First quarter, (165). Caracas: Centro Gumilla. 38–47.
——— (2017). Las nociones de fuentes y autoría en la información periodística dedicada a la cultura. In *Innovación, tecnologías e información. El nuevo paisaje de la Comunicación. Memorias arbitradas del VI Congreso de Investigadores Venezolanos de la Comunicación (Invecom)*. Caracas: Universidad Monteávila, pp. 51–66. Retrieved June 29, 2018, from https://es.scribd.com/document/412669489/Libro-arbitrado-VI-Congreso-Invecom

IPYS-Venezuela. (December 12, 2019). Intercortados 2019: censura masiva en Venezuela. Retrieved January 30, 2019, from https://ipysvenezuela. org/2019/12/12/intercortados-2019-censura-masiva-en-venezuela/

Kovach, B., & Rosenstiel, T. (2004). *Los elementos del periodismo*. Colombia: Ediciones El País-Santillana.

Kozak Rovero, G. (2015). Revolución Bolivariana: políticas culturales en la Venezuela socialista de Hugo Chávez. *Cuadernos de Literatura*, January-June, *XIX* (37), 38–56.

Martín Barbero, J. (1991). Dinámicas urbanas de la cultura. *Gaceta de Colcultura*, (12), December. Retrieved February 3, 2000, from https://red. pucp.edu.pe/wp-content/uploads/biblioteca/080908.pdf

Martini, S. (2000). *Periodismo, noticia y noticiabilidad*. Colombia: Grupo Editorial Norma.

Miranda, J. (1996). "Panorama de las revistas culturales venezolanas, 1970–1990." In *América: Cahiers du CRICCAL*, (5–16). Le discours culturel dans les revues latino-américaines, 1970–1990, pp. 231–36. Retrieved July 12, 2000, from https://www.persee.fr/doc/ameri_0982-9237_1996_num_15_1_1193

Paone, M. (March 2, 2015). "La primavera de los medios digitales en Venezuela." *El País*. Retrieved March 3, 2015, from https://elpais.com/internacional/2015/03/01/actualidad/1425228969_135730.html

Pulido, J. (August 5, 2019). La cultura como periódico. En los 76 años de *El Nacional*: 3 de agosto de 2019. *Crear en Salamanca*. Retrieved August 6, 2019, from http://www.crearensalamanca.com/la-cultura-como-periodico-en-los-76-anos-de-el-nacional-3-de-agosto-de-1943-2019-por-jose-pulido/?fbclid=IwAR2hoMSBAVuy2gc_fNAFPk_WBqrXdSe8xMn6aAM-nIkFnGG0MswHS57JVtig

Quiñones, R. (2008). Mapa de la situación de la prensa y medios regionales. *Revista Comunicación*, (144), October-December, 84–98.

Ramos, M. E. (August 18, 2019). La cultura en Venezuela: notas sobre el desmontaje y la resistencia. *Papel Literario, El Nacional*, pp. 4 and 5. Retrieved August 18, 2019, from https://www.elnacional.com/papel-literario/la-cultura-en-venezuela-notas-sobre-el-desmontaje-y-la-resistencia/

Rivera, J. (2003). *El periodismo cultural*. Buenos Aires: Paidós.

Safar, Elizabeth (2013). El Aló Presidente y las cadenas de radio y televisión. Espejo de la pasión autoritaria del presidente Chávez. In Bisbal, M. (Ed.), *Saldo en Rojo. Comunicaciones y cultura en la Era Bolivariana*. Caracas: Universidad Católica Andrés Bello-Konrad Adenauer Stiftung, pp. 226–49.

Silva-Ferrer, M. (2013). Migraciones culturales en los 14 años de Hugo Chávez. In Bisbal, M. (Ed.), *Saldo en Rojo. Comunicaciones y cultura en la Era Bolivariana*. Caracas: Universidad Católica Andrés Bello-Konrad Adenauer Stiftung, pp. 274–92.

——— (2017). *El cuerpo dócil de la cultura. Poder, cultura y comunicación en la Venezuela de Chávez*. Caracas: AB Ediciones de la Universidad Católica Andrés Bello- Iberoamericana Vervuert.

Unesco (2009). Alianza Global para la diversidad cultural. El ciclo cultural. Retrieved July 13, 2012, from http://www.unesco.org/new/es/culture/themes/cultural-diversity/cultural-expressions/programmes/global-alliance-for-cultural-diversity/culture-cycle/

Urribarrí, R. (2013). ¿Medios alternativos? ¿Se buscan! In Bisbal, M. (Ed.), *Saldo en Rojo. Comunicaciones y cultura en la Era Bolivariana.* Caracas: Universidad Católica Andrés Bello-Konrad Adenauer Stiftung, pp. 68–85.

Weffer, L. (January 15, 2007). "El socialismo necesita una hegemonía comunicacional." Andrés Izarra Interview. *El Nacional*, p. A-4.

Index

Note: *Italic* page numbers refer to figures and page numbers followed by "n" denote endnotes.

"Aburrimiento y Autoritarismo. Selfiementary #1: crisis del billete de BsF. 100 (22-12-2016)" 23
Acción Democrática (AD) 91
Acosta, Y. 83
advertising: "Advertiser State" 4, 77, 83; and collective imaginaries 83–7; and investment 80–3; and power 80–3
Agencia Venezolana de Noticias 99
ALBA Audiovisual Production Plan 22
Alba Ciudad 127
Aló Presidente television program 81, 96, 97, 109
Alterio, Hector 12
Álvarez Marcano, Luis 11
Álvarez, Mariano 12
Anderson, B. 121
Anti-Hatred Law 34
Aporrea.org 99
Arab Spring 21
Arvelo, Alberto 11, 16–17
Así Somos 128
ÁvilaTV 99, 127

Bachelet, Michelle 92
Barre, Albert Désiré 9
Benacerraf, Margot 22
Bicentennial Bank 82
Bigott magazine 125
Bisbal, Marcelino 127
Black Lives Matter 43
bland storylines and absence of contemporary topics 65–7
Blasetti, Alessandro 11
Bolívar, Simón 5, 8, 84, 127; cinematic representations of 9–14; feature films that include portrayals of *12*; Hugo Chávez dubbed as 8–9; overview 8–9
"Bolivarian Cultural Revolution" 121
Bolivarian Revolution 22, 90, 93–4, 95, 98, 106, 107, 110–11, 115, 132
"The Bolivarian Revolution's Troll Army" 39

Cabello, Diosdado 111
Cabral, Manuel 11
Cabrera, Ángel 26
Cadena Capriles 69
Cadenas, Margarita 22–3
Cadena Tres (Mexico) 61, 64
Caldera, Rafael 108, 126
Cañizález, Andrés 92, 132
Capriles Radonski, Henrique 35, 47–8
Caracas Athenaeum radio 126
Carmona, Pedro 92
Carrera Damas, Germán 10
Castro, Fidel 111
Catholic Church 91
Caudillos and digital age 90–102
censorship 3–4, 23, 28, 32, 34, 36, 38, 85, 100–1, 106, 120, 129
Cervecería Regional 81
César, Julio 94

Index

Chacón, Rufo 116
Chávez, Hugo 1–2, 61, 63, 64, 65, 79–80; 21st century socialism, promoted by 81; administration and cinema 21; August 2004 recall referendum of 65; and "Bolivarian Revolution" 107–8; and *Correo del Orinoco* 127; and coup d'état of April 11, 2002 92; death of 14, 47; dubbed as Simón Bolívar 8–9; gaze in everyday life 117–18; icon of Chávez's eyes and Maduro 116–17; and media 3; and "personalism" 97; RCG implemented by 79, 81, 83; second term as competitive authoritarianism 33; strategies for eroding democracy 32; touch 115–16; *see also* Chavismo
Chávezcadanga Mission 39
Chavismo 1–2, 34–5, 42, 90–102, 115; achieving *Media Caesarism* 96–101; and *Bolívar, el hombre de las dificultades* 15–16; construction of a new hegemony 93–6; hegemony halfway 101–2; and media 3; overview 91–3; Twitter strategy 39; *see also* Chávez, Hugo
Chavista Revolution 115
Chavista socialism 118
Circuit of Culture 62
CiudadCcs 128
Civil Resistance Campaign 23
cluster analysis 56
Cochino Pop 129
Coetzee, John Maxwell 101
Colgate Palmolive 81
collective imaginaries and advertising 83–7
Comisión Nacional de Telecomunicaciones (CONATEL) 38, 66, 69, 71n17, 101
Comité de Organización Política Electoral Independiente (COPEI) 91
"Communicating State" 82
communication: government political 79; and hegemony 121–2; and media 121–2
communicational hegemony 33–5, 47–50, 69, 80, 92–3, 96, 99, 115, 122, 127

competitive authoritarianism 33
Complejo Editorial Maneiro 124
Consejo Nacional de la Cultura (CONAC) 122
Corporación Maneiro 70
Corporación Venezolana de Televisión (VTV) 99
Correo del Orinoco 99, 127
Cortés, A. 78
Cresta Metálica 129
cultural diffusion in Venezuelan media 120–33
cultural information in public media 126–8
cultural journalism: from high culture to media culture 120–1; print 123–4; resistance and reinvention 132–3
culture: Aníbal Ford's definition of 120–1; high 120–1; highbrow 122–5; lack in electronic media 125–6; media 120–1
cyberactivism 2.0 21
cyber politics, with WhatsApp 55–8, 56–8

Datanálisis 71n6
death and reinvention of media 125
"Democratic Caesarism" 94
Democratic Unity Table (MUD) 50
democratization 46–7
Díaz, Simón 26
digital media 133; Digital Media Directory 129; native 132–3; reach and consumption of 132
documentaries 22–3; *Araya* 22; *3 Bellezas* 23; *Bloques* 23; *Estátodo bien* 23; *La ciudad que nosve* 22; *La estrategia del azar* 23; *La Familia* 22; *La librería* 26; *Macuro, la fuerza de un pueblo* 26; *Maracaibo con vista al lago* 23; *Nocturno* 23; *Pozo muerto* 22; "¿Quésomos?" 26; *Selfiementary* 23–5, 28; "Somoslibres" 26; "Somosmás" 25–8; "Somostodo/Somostodos" 26; *Tarde de machos* 23
"¿Dónde está la revolución?" 26
Dragnic, Olga 121
Dudamel, Gustavo 86

EBR-200 8
Eco, Umberto 114
economic constraints
El Carabobeño 125
El Cautivo 129
El Correo del Orinoco 128
El culto a Bolívar (Carrera Damas) 10
electronic media: lack of culture in 125–6; and Law RESORTE 34
El Impulso 125
El Nacional 122–4
El-Teatro 129
El Universal 34, 69, 122, 124, 125
Emisora Cultural de Caracas 126
Empresas Polar 81
Enlightenment 121
Escalona, José Simón 64
Esfera Cultural 129
Espacio Público 124

Facebook 21, 40
fascism 2, 96
Federación de Cámaras y Asociaciones de Comercio y Producción de Venezuela (Fedecámaras) 91
Fernández, Carmen Beatriz 125
Fiallo, Delia 63, 71n3
film industry: cinematic representations of Simón Bolívar 9–14; complexities in Venezuela 7–8; Venezuela 5
films 7–18, 20–8; *Bolívar, el hombre de las dificultades* 7–8, 11, 15–18; *Bolívar, the hero* 11; *Bolívar, tropikal symphony* 11; *Bolívar soy yo!* 11; *Femmes du chaos vénézuélien* 22–3; *Manuela Sáenz* 12; *Miranda Returns* 12; *Pelo Malo* 22; *Piedra, papel, tijera* 26; *The Saint of the Sword* 11; *Simón Bolívar* 11, 12, 13
Flores, María Antonieta 129
Flores, Maria Fernanda 51
Ford, Aníbal 120
Fourth Republic 94, 102
Fujimori, Alberto 59
Fundación Villa del Cine 21–2

García, M. 4, 77
García Canclini, Néstor 121

García Riera, Emilio 13
Gardner, Howard 14
Global Inventory of Organized Social Media Manipulation 38
Globovisión 34, 69, 95
Gómez, Juan Vicente 63, 71n5, 94–5
Gómez Jiménez, Jorge 128
Government Communication Routines (RCG) 77, 79–80, 83
"Government diffuser Propaganda" 79, 82
Gramsci, Antonio 91, 94, 122
"Graphic Image of the Bolivarian Government of Venezuela of Basic Applications" 84
Great Housing Mission Venezuela 82
Guaidó, Juan 42–3
Guédez, Jesús Enrique 22
Güerere, Abdel 61
Guerrero, Gustavo 26
Gutiérrez, Pedro Elías 86
Guzmán Blanco, Antonio 9

Hahn, K. S. 53
hegemony: changing 90–102; construction of a new 93–6; halfway 101–2; and media 121–2
highbrow culture 122–5; and the massive industrial 122–5
high culture 120–1
Historia documental del cine mexicano (García Riera) 13
Hitler, Adolf 97
Hueck, Alfredo 23
Hugo Rafael Chávez Frías *see* Chávez, Hugo
Human Rights Watch 65

iconicity 112–14
"imagined communities" 121
Instagram 40–1
Institute of Press and Society Venezuela (IPYS) 100); IPYS-Venezuela 124
Inter-American Court of Human Rights 71n7
Inter-American Human Rights System 99
internet control 36–8

investment: and advertising 80–3; and power 80–3
Iyengar, S. 53
Izaguirre, Rodolfo 10, 11
Izarra, Andrés 80, 122

Jabés, Hernán 5, 23, 25–8
Jencquel, Tuki 23

Kim Jong-un 97
Kovach, B. 133

La Dueña 63
Lafourcade, Natalia 26
"La marcha del Primero de Mayo fue acorralada. Selfiementary # 10: Crisis en Venezuela" 25
Lamata Torres, Luis Alberto 11, 12, 16, 18
La Radio del Sur 127
La Revuelta 128
La Roca de Crear 128
Letralia, Tierra de Letras 128
Ley de Responsabilidad Social en Radio y Televisión (Law of Social Responsibility for Radio and Television, Ley RESORTE) 65, 69
The Liberator 7–8, 11, 17–18
Librería Sónica 125
López, Leopoldo 37
Los Pasos Perdidos 125

Maduro, Nicolás 5, 7, 14, 17, 22, 26, 34, 41–3, 61, 66, 80, 82, 85, 90, 92, 94, 97, 102, 106, *107,* 110–11, 115–16; and communication hegemony 48; taking over presidency 47–8; use of cable television industry 49
manipulation: influence and 111–12; persuasion for 111–12
Martín Barbero, Jesús 121
Martini, S. 133
massive industrial and highbrow culture 122–5
Massive Magazine System *(Sistema Masivo de Revistas)* 128
media: and communication 121–2; contextual elements 121–2; death and reinvention of 125; and hegemony 121–2

Media Caesarism 90–102; achieving 96–101
Media Certification Committee of the National Association of Advertisers (ANDA) 80
media culture 120–1
Medina Angarita, Isaías 13
Memorias de Venezuela 128
Mi Film 13
Mijares, V. 35
Ministry of Communication and Information (MINCI) 22, 80, 82, 127
MIPCOM 65, 71n14
Miranda, Julio 125
Montero, Carlos Caridad 5, 23–5, 28
Morris, C. 106, 113–14
Muñoz, Boris 94
Mussolini, Benito 97
"Myth of Government" 4, 77

National Dialogue Roundtable parties 42
National Film Platform 21
National Integrated Service for the Administration of Customs Duties and Taxes (SENIAT) 81
National Telephone Company of Venezuela (CANTV) 81
Navarrete, Rodrigo 109
Nazis 96
neo-authoritarian communication control model 33–5
Neruda, Pablo 16
"new communicational architecture" 125
newspapers 48, 70, 80–1, 92, 100, 121, 123–5, 132
Nielsen 71n6
900 pánico 26
#NoEnMiNombre 42
Noti-Tarde 34

opposition filmmaking 20–3
Ortega, E. 78
Orwell, George 114, 117

Pacto de Punto Fijo 91
Padrón, Leonardo 66–7
Palma, Héctor 12
Panorama 100–1, 125

Para vertemejor 64
parliamentary election (2015) 50–5
"patriotic hacking" 37
Peirce, Charles Sanders 106, 113
Pérez, Carlos Andrés 63, 85, 108
Pérez Jiménez, Marcos 63, 71n4
Petróleos de Venezuela, S.A. (PDVSA) 81–2
Pineda, A. 79
A Plena Voz 128
Poder Vivir 128
populism 46–7
power: and advertising 80–3; and investment 80–3
press: between highbrow culture and massive industrial 122–5; print 81, 100–1, 128
Procter & Gamble 81
Prodavinci 124
production values, lagging 67–8
Propagandistic Institutional Advertising 79
"Protesta nocturna por los caídos. Selfiementary #17. Caracas, 17 de mayo de 2017" 25
public media 126–8

Radio Caracas Televisión (RCTV) 3, 61, 63–4, 66, 68, 95); Coral Pictures 63
Radio Nacional de Venezuela 99, 127
Ramírez, Edgar 7, 11
Ramírez, Leo 111
Ramos, Julio 11
RCTV *see* Radio Caracas Televisión (RCTV)
Rebolledo, Carlos 22
reinvention: online 128–32; resistance and 132–3
resistance and reinvention 120–33, 132–3
RESORTE law 34
RESORTE-ME law 34
Revista OJO 129
Revolución Bolivariana 8
Rey, J. 79
Rincón, Guillermo 11
Riorda, M. 4, 77, 79
Rísquez, Diego 12
Rodríguez, Jorge 128
Rodríguez, Simón 8

Romero, C. 83
Rondón, Gustavo 22
Rondón, Mariana 22
Rosenstiel, T. 133
RTI (Colombia) 64

Safar, Elizabeth 121
"Sala de Prensa Unidad" 51
Salas, Javier 82
Samet, Robert 15, 18
Schell, Maximilian 11
Semanario Cultural de Venezuela 128
Sembramedia 129
Se Mueve 128
SIBCI (Bolivarian System of Communication and Information) 127–8
Silva-Ferrer, M. 122
Simón Bolívar National Project 47, 84
Simón Bolívar Youth Orchestra 86
social media 4; contested spaces and Venezuelan government 38–42; information warfare in 38–42
Soler, Julián 11, 13
"Soviet Enlightenment" 96
Soviet Revolution 96
Spear, Mónica 66
Stalin, Joseph 97
"the Star Wars plot" 14
State communications apparatus 107
State-Communicator model 33
Straka, Tomás 7, 14, 17
Strategic Center for Security and Protection of the Homeland (CESPPA) 37

technical censorship 36–8
Telemundo (USA) 61, 64, 72n21; Telemundo telenovelas 68
telenovelas 5; *Amor Secreto* 64; *Chepe Fortuna* 66; *Corazón Esmeralda* 64; *Cosita Rica* 65; *Cristal* 63; *de época* 63; *de ruptura* 62, 63; *De todasmaneras Rosa* 64; *Entre tu amor y mi amor* 64; *Esmeralda* 63; *Estefanía* 63; *Kassandra* 63; *La Reina del Sur* 72n21; narconovelas 66, 71n16; *Por estascalles* 63; *rosa* 62, 65, 70; Telemundo telenovelas 68; *Tomasa Tequiero* 71n15; "universal telenovela" 68

Telesur 127
Televen 61, 64
Televisa (Mexico) 64, 69
television 3, 24, 34–5, 48–9, 61, 65–9, 78–82, 95–7, 108–9, 125–8, 133
Todos Adentro 128
"Tonada de Luna Llena" 26
Torre, Leopoldo 11–12
Torres, Contreras 13
Torres, Diego Rísquez 11
Tráfico Visual 129
Triana, Jorge Alí 11
Trump, Donald J. 96
#TrumpHandsOffVenezuela 43
TVes 61, 99
Twitter 4, 21, 40, 42
tyrannization: defined 46; and Venezuela 46–7

Últimas Noticias 34, 69, 125
Urribarrí, R. 128

Valero, Roque 11
Vale TV 126
Vallenilla Lanz, Laureano 94–5
Veintiuno magazine 125
Venevision 61, 63–4, 66
Venezolana de Televisión 126
Venezuela: Chavismo (*see* Chavismo); film industry 5; information warfare 42–3; parliamentary election (2015) 50–5; penetration of pay TV in *49*; platform by political preferences *53*; polarization 14–15; political process 1; populist regime 5; pro-democratization forces 41; status of institutional advertising during 1999–2018 77–87; telenovelas 5
Venezuelan Advertising Agency (AVP) 82
Venezuelan Advertising Institute of Caracas (IVP) 80
Venezuelan Federation of Advertising Agencies (FEVAP) 80; ANDA-Fevap Media Certification Committee report 81
Venezuelan filmmakers: opposition filmmaking 20–3; video activism 20–3

Venezuelan government: and contested media spaces 32–43; neo-authoritarian communication control model 33–5; second-generation internet control 36–8; and social media contested spaces 38–42; and technical censorship 36–8
"Venezuelan Heart" ("Corazón Venezolano") campaign 84
Venezuelan journalism 120
Venezuelan media: cultural diffusion in 120–33; cultural information in public media 126–8; cultural journalism 120–1; death and reinvention of media 125; highbrow culture and massive industrial 122–5; from high culture to media culture 120–1; lack of culture in electronic media 125–6; media, communication, and hegemony 121–2; overview 120; the press 122–5; reinvention online 128–32; resistance and reinvention 132–3
Venezuelan political communication 106–18; analysis of the icon 114–15; Chávez's eyes, icon of, and Maduro 116–17; Chávez's gaze in everyday life 117–18; Chávez's touch 115–16; iconic and iconicity 112–14; influence and persuasion for manipulation 111–12; overview 106–7; theoretical and referential framework 107–11
Venezuelan telenovelas 61–70; assumptions and choices 68–9; bland storylines and absence of contemporary topics 65–7; lagging production values 67–8; overview 61–2; from protagonist to extra 65; from riches to rags 69–70; then and now 62–5; theoretical framework and methods 62
Venpres 98
Vera-Villanueva, Henrique 11
Verismo 70n2
Vertov, Dziga 21
video activism 20–3
Vinogradoff, Ludmila 110
ViveTV 99, 127

Wallis, M. 113–14
Warner Brothers 10
Wessels, J. 21
"What Have They Done to Liberty, That I Do Not Know You?" 26
WhatsApp 4, 41, 125; cyber politics 2020 with 55–8, *56–8*; political messaging by Venezuelans on 54–5, *55*; use in protests 54; use in tyrannized society 46–59
"The Wonderful Lamp" (Buxo) 110

YouTube 21, 51, *52*
YVKE Mundial 127

Zamora, Ezequiel 8, 85

Taylor & Francis eBooks

www.taylorfrancis.com

A single destination for eBooks from Taylor & Francis with increased functionality and an improved user experience to meet the needs of our customers.

90,000+ eBooks of award-winning academic content in Humanities, Social Science, Science, Technology, Engineering, and Medical written by a global network of editors and authors.

TAYLOR & FRANCIS EBOOKS OFFERS:

- A streamlined experience for our library customers
- A single point of discovery for all of our eBook content
- Improved search and discovery of content at both book and chapter level

REQUEST A FREE TRIAL
support@taylorfrancis.com

For Product Safety Concerns and Information please contact our EU representative GPSR@taylorandfrancis.com
Taylor & Francis Verlag GmbH, Kaufingerstraße 24, 80331 München, Germany

www.ingramcontent.com/pod-product-compliance
Lightning Source LLC
Chambersburg PA
CBHW071822230426
43670CB00013B/2534